WHY SHOULDN'T I CALL MY SON CLINT?

David Hocking

PUBLISHING
www.vividpublishing.com.au

© 2011 David Hocking

Published by VIVID Publishing
P.O. Box 948, Fremantle
Western Australia 6959
www.vividpublishing.com.au
2nd Edition - International

National Library of Australia Cataloguing-in-Publication
Author: Hocking, David, 1968-
Title: Why shouldn't I call my son Clint? / David Hocking.
ISBN: 9780980545937 (pbk.)
Subjects: Names, Personal--Psychological aspects.
            Personality.
Dewey Number: 929.4

No part of this publication may be translated, reproduced, or transmitted in any form or by any means, in whole or in part, electronic or mechanical including photocopying, recording, or by any information storage or retrieval system without prior permission in writing from the copyright owner. The views expressed in this book are not necessarily those of the publisher.

For more information on this book and the author,

visit www.thenametheory.com

"Well some girls'd giggle and I'd get red,
and some guy'd laugh and I'd,
bust his head.

I tell ya,
life ain't easy for a boy named Sue."

Johnny Cash (1932-2003)

INTRO-DUCTION

At some point, a few years ago, I began to see some marked similarities in people who shared the same name and I arrived at a rather surprising question: *What if your name says everything about you?*

Imagine if you or your spouse gave birth to a baby girl, and that your partner insisted she be called Dirt. How do you think you'd react?

So, how is it that names make a difference? Why do people change them, and why do movie stars take on a pseudonym?

The answer might be very simple: if something looks good we tend to think it is good. In the case of what we are called, a name is like a tiny piece of personalised music that, like any tune, people react to in a natural and completely subconscious way. Your name, therefore, arguably functions as a small noise diagram that describes who you are, what you're like and what you might be capable of. For instance, some names are smooth and sexy, rolling off the tongue as easily as dropping a ball onto a padded floor, while others force you to constrict parts of your face and throat awkwardly just so you can spit them out of your mouth. And our subconscious is there the whole time, analysing and computing how easy a name is to deal with, and using the substantial bulk of our human imagination to do so.

Julius Caesar said it best: *if the whole world deems a man to be of a particular nature, then he will become that man.* It's human nature. Have you ever stopped to think how the world might predict you?

So, this book is an attempt to qualify about 2000 names metaphorically or otherwise – depending on the name – and there are some points to remember.

Firstly, because of our accent and the way we live and operate, this book is probably only applicable in Australia.

Secondly, each name description is intended exactly for that name. If your name is Robert but the whole world has always known you as Rob, then the long version will be of little use to you, or to someone who wants to look-up Rob, even though there are often obvious relationships between related names.

Another phenomenon is that frequently, but not always, there are important differences between names that sound the same yet are spelt differently. It's a complicated explanation but, basically, that's just how it is.

The final thing to remember is that surnames have a huge affect on first names and so there are obvious limitations in trying to describe individuals without them. Some might say it is impossible, and I basically agree, but what the hell.....

In any case, girls names are in the front half, boys in the back, all alphabetically listed, and I wish you good luck!

David Hocking.

FEMALE

*"Women have a much better time
than men in this world.
There are far more things
forbidden to them."*

Oscar Wilde.

Ab: Ab is what Abby turns into after the day is done, and when she can put her feet up and relax.

Abigail: 'The Abigail' is a prawn trawler built for a purpose and not for speed or adulation.

Abby: Whether she's your teacher, work colleague, wife, lover, mother or friend, Abby is unavoidable and inevitable, and for all the right reasons.

Adelaide: A banshee before she was born, Adelaide is the life of the party on a good day and a dangerous psychopath on a bad one.

Adele: Something in her name throws her way out there, almost beyond reach and nearly completely isolated. But, once you get there Adele is lovely, and sensual, and intelligent, and funny, and anyone who knows her could go on and on.....

Adriana: The B-grade actress who is happy enough to work on Days of Our Lives for 10 years. Yeah, she's a bit of a prima donna but deep down she's pretty chilled out, and so long as she's somewhere near the centre of attention she's happy enough.

Adrienne: Does anyone really know her? She's intelligent, she's normal but, let's face it, she's not the most interesting organism on the planet.

Ag: Ag speaks the truth, she's funny and overall she's bloody good value but she is about as prissy and sensitive as the Tanami Desert in the middle of January.

Agata: Agata sees passed all bullshit, her laughter is never false, she does what she says she's going to do and she secretly weeps the tears of the stratosphere when she hears of the suffering of those she doesn't even know.

Agatha: A busybody. A stickybeak. A cooker of cakes.

3

♀ FEMALE

Aicha: ....Bless you! Have you got a cold? Can I get you some tissues?

Aimee: A howling drunk, and not the wailing damsel in distress, drunk. More like the howling at the moon like a fucking werewolf, drunk. Maybe she's a Kiwi? (Apologies if she isn't.)

Ainslea: Ainslea is intensely loyal. Her conservative skin hides a core that is ready to burst into song at any moment.

Aisha: Another modern girl who does what she needs to do although she does seem to do well at squeezing the most from a situation. She'd be great to have around if your washing machine decided to spit the dummy and the sodden towels needed to be wrung out, manually.

Akiko: The gorgeous Kyoto rebel.

Alana: Alana rhymes with A Good Lie Down. She'd love to be viewed as being mysterious and sexually exotic – who doesn't? – and when she's on her own she absolutely is.

Aleca: The nonchalant chip off the old block whose refreshing and unexpected ways belie her inner drive. She's smart, but she's not a smart-arse.

Alecia: Alecia fully intends to pursue a career on television; in front of the camera, not behind it.

Alex: Alex is a control freak and the name of a roll of barbed wire. Sexy, yes, intelligent, yes, but rile her at your peril!

Alexandra: 'Where's my pony, mother? I WANT MY PONY!!'

Alexis: Alexis is the sensation you feel when you hop into an old Mercedes with dodgy suspension, and drive fast along a heavily corrugated road.

4

FEMALE ♀

Ali: A listener, a teller and the fulcrum and shock absorber of any mechanical or chaotic system, though she may be a tremendous energy generator in her own right. (eg. like the giant red storm on Jupiter that enables the rest of the atmosphere of the gas giant to be relatively stable).

Alice: Razor sharp, relaxed and adventurous all at once. Nothing gets passed this girl.

Alicia: A walking dichotomy: Apart from being sexy and intelligent, she has a huge ego that requires lots of maintenance yet she knows, and has an interest in, nearly everyone. She's cool in a crisis but then again she'll fly off the handle if she discovers that someone else has been using her hairbrush. And if she takes a dislike to you, then you'll never hear the daggers being thrust into your back.

Alison: Alison gives people the benefit of the doubt unless they're obvious fools, in which case she'll nod politely, above the table, while tapping the foot of her husband/boyfriend/partner beneath it. Indeed, Alison is contained yet not reluctant.

Aliya: ....bullshit. She couldn't lie to save her life.

Allanah: See Alana.

Allegra: The magic elixir of seduction.

Alleni: The gorgeous little nymph from the island of Crete, in the Mediterranean Sea. She's funny, she's happy and she's delightfully unpredictable.

Allison: See Alison.

♀ **FEMALE**

Ally: The sensual analyser who understands the bigger picture, as well as endeavouring to seek answers to those questions that arise from behind the scenes. It's a busy life but somehow she manages to keep it all together and retain her rather cool (if not occasionally secretive-looking) exterior.

Allycat: The name of a stunning Blue Russian who is in full heat.

Alyssa: Alyssa is the sound of a marlin fin slicing through the surface of the sea. A beautiful creation of nature, the great fish is curvy and sexy but not if it leaps into the boat. (You hear about this happening occasionally.)

Amanda: Your mouth stays open at the end of saying her name, and this is the preamble to discovering how delicious and rare she really is. *What is it about Amanda?*

Amber: Amber has $10,000 boobs, wears an incredibly tight skirt and charges between $300 and $800 per hour – depending on the weather and how busy it is.

Ambrosia: Ambrosia is over-flowing like a glass that has had too much coke poured into it, too quickly. For a second it looks delicious and exciting, until the reality of the situation dawns on you and you are faced with little to drink and a mess.

Amelia: As a vast expanse of North Australian desert, Amelia rhymes with "Aaah, Christ it's hot..."
Not much grows there and not much wants to. If you intend to visit I'd take plenty of water and definitely tell someone where you're headed. Bon voyage.

Amelie: Great things are always expected of her, and that is always possible, but Amelie is actually quite shy.

Amera: Seductive, refined and mysterious, Amera incites wonder and intrigue in all those that meet her. Men want to gobble her up and women want to know how she does it.

Amie: Not as charismatic as her more gorgeous and volatile cousin (Amy), Amie is a good soul full of decent causes and fun-loving desires, although she more fearful of death and/or some kind of public embarrassment.

Amity: Conscientious.

Amy: Beautiful and sensitive, Amy rides a motorbike, rolls a mean joint, does a thousand things at once and often has far too much energy for any man to catch. If only they were so lucky.

Ana: With a personality that could easily be described as crisp, Ana is slightly unfinished and as a result she needs and/or wants more attention than most.

Anaxe: Weird name, amazing girl. If she isn't donking saltwater crocodiles on the head with a special saltwater crocodile donking stick, she's telling jokes while making sandwiches. Anaxe.

Anchalee: Anchalee has a Thai/European heritage which provides her with a wise head. For instance, she flies to Bangkok to get her hair and eye lashes done and by doing so, saves a packet. Cost: Hair $850 (plus extensions), lashes $150.

Andrea: Andrea says the following phrases quite often:
'No! Not again!'
'Oh, look, I'm so sorry! Oh dear!'
'Have you got insurance?'

Andrine: Andrine knows how to prioritise. If she is going on a camping trip in her new four-wheel drive, for example, and she is trying, unsuccessfully, to fit a super-frozen bag of ice into the esky that happens to be next to the car, she will instinctively wrench the bag from the vessel and swing it against the vehicle, slamming it against the fresh duco in order to break up the ice so it can fit around the beer.

Anetta: Fun-loving and frivolous, Anetta is angered only by boredom.

Anette: See Annette.

Ang': Good old Ang'. The remnants of the chaotic Angela, Angel and Angeline loom large on her horizon but when she's here, Ang is more relaxed than anywhere and certainly good fun to have around. Watch out for that repressed temper, although...

Angel: She is the only person that matters and as such she is a walking disaster.

Angela: The Angela is the act of colliding your little toe into the bottom corner of a cupboard that you happen to be walking past. Great fun.

Angeline: The Angeline is the name of the expression that develops on your face after you eat a large spoonful of delicious-looking strawberry yoghurt that, after increasing seconds, you realize is probably off. Indeed, it might be very off.

Angie: Placid on the outside, fiery as hell in the middle.

Anika: The black sheep of any family whose foul moods are worse and more tempestuous than most. Boys are crazy about her but are never sure how to approach her.

Anita: Anita is an honest if not deceptively restless soul who leaves many tasks in her life slightly unfinished.

Anja: "Come on," she says playfully. "Hurry up. I don't want to be late!"
She doesn't say it because she's antsy about getting there on time, just because she loves life – loves all the big, fun, social bits – and wants to share in it as much as she can before she gets old.

Anje: Anje has it 'goin on' in all areas, and she's not to be taken lightly (or messed with, for that matter).

Anjuli: The Sexy Clown. She has a degree in psychology, music and economic management and no one knows how she fits it all together.

Anki: Anki is open and thoughtful, sensual and unusual, and as a living embodiment of some kind of night-fairy, we always expect that weird and wonderful little coincidences will occur whenever she's around. Maybe she's another good witch?

Anmaree: The name of a stainless steel commercial juicer in any health food shop. Some days she might be overly temperamental, groaning at length about the littlest thing and threatening to tear your fingers off if you so much as look at her, while other days, just when you least expect it, she's the one that comes to the fore when the chips are down and when the day needs to be saved by someone. (She looks great when she isn't stressed.) Anyway, what day is it?

♀ FEMALE

Anmarie: See Anmaree.

Anna: Inside the boundaries of correct behaviour she's a picture of neatness, loveliness and calm. Outside it, she's a sensual and charismatic wildcard who is capable of nearly anything. So, who's in the room?

Annabel: Never thin. Rarely dim.

Annabelle: The Melodramatic Actress.

Annalea: Annalea is a dynamic and gorgeous woman. She's read every book and seen every movie, she can act as well as the best of them and she's make a perfect drama lecturer. In fact, where is she?

Annalise: Initially she may seem quite proper and posh but she isn't, really. She is, in fact, very natural and she has classic looks that force the husbands in the boardroom to wish they were very single.

Anna-Marie: See Anmaree.

Anne: Regimented and organised, Anne is God-fearing 59% of the time.

Anneliese: The American president Roosevelt once said, "Give a lazy man a job and he'll find an easy way to do it," and this applies to Anneliese, perfectly. She's got street smarts, man smarts and life skills that enable her to live her life well, and with a smile on her dial.

Anne-Marie: See Anmaree.

Annette: An interesting person; an interesting phenomenon - that being, when string, nylon or any kind of rope tangles up into an irretrievable disaster. A good example is that of a parachutist who leaps from a plane, pulls the rip-chord and then falls to their death as they try and spread apart the shrouds that have mortally tangled.

Annie: The naughty little sister. Quick to arrive and quick to leave, frisky Annie lives a busy life although no one is ever sure where she is at any given time.

Annmarie: See Anmaree.

Ann-Marie: See Anmaree.

Ansu: Thoughtful. Sexy. Cool.

Ansuya: As a lovely psychiatrist she will often ask the question, 'What's it to ya'?', although in a very non-threatening manner. (She actually asks herself the same question, all day long.)

Anthea: Anthea is the sponge cake that never rose and is now out the back being eaten by the dog. Don't assume, therefore, that she isn't maximally lovable, and for the right reasons.

Antoinette: Very well travelled, Antoinette enjoys intrigue in a relationship, she's disappointed by cheap red and she delights in floral bath salts.

Apple: Naive.

♀ FEMALE

April: April will do whatever she can to ensure than she and her family always give a good impression of themselves, and regardless if she is the daughter, the mother, the aunty or the grandmother.

Arabella: The gorgeous princess in a mystical land. Legend has it that she can drink anyone under the table, and that she has actually killed men in bed.

Ari: As the full spinnaker of a multi-million dollar maxi-yacht that's leading the fleet up the Derwent, Ari drives the vessel like it's nothing at all, and she does it with a sensual and easy poise that comforts and encourages all those behind her, on board, who would be completely screwed without her.

Ariel: Ariel is the real name of a huge gold statue of the Buddha. She is all-knowing, fun-loving, truth-seeking and a sage that everyone is happy to be near and learn from.

Ash: Blue sky.

Asha: The shape and sound of a sleek and sexy arrowhead whistling through the air. A great way to live. A great way to die.

Ashley: Contorted up inside herself, Ashley is a pretty girl who worries too much about trivial things.

Astrid: A Swedish-German Princess who rides a late model BMW motorbike, wears a short hairdo and is completely gay.

Athena: As the ex-Queen of a lost civilization, Athena was re-incarnated into this life as a well-made and expensive bell around a healthy cow's neck. She now makes a wonderful noise that sounds a bit too dopy to take seriously.

Audrey: An English Literature graduate who lost her virginity way too late. But that's okay because she now makes a wonderful older lover.

Ava: In theory, Ava is dramatic and unselfconscious but, in reality, she is more measured and fretful than you'd reckon.

Ayda: Ayda carries certain responsibilities that weigh her down from time to time, but she listens to people and she's friendly.

Ayema: Similar to Amen, Ayema is what you say when you arrive at a tranquil water hole after a three day trek through northern Pakistan. What a wonderful vision she is.

B: B takes no shit from anyone or anything and she gets on with it, having as much well-earned fun on the way as is possible within the constraints of the situation.

Babs: Rarely rushing to a decision or a point of view, Babs surveys the scene in second gear for most of the time, moving and thinking with an easy style. When she decides to act, however, you will definitely know about it.

♀ FEMALE

Barbara: A sensual women who has travelled the world. In wintertime she wears an exquisite woollen scarf that she tosses around her neck with the grace of movement that one would see in a stallion's tail if at a gentle canter.

Bea: See B.

Beate: Patient and never intrusive, Beate possesses a lovely calming aspect.

Beatrice: Beatrice hasn't had an orgasm for about 15 years, not even by herself. Not that it matters, really, because she's passed all that bullshit.

Bec: Yep, smart, savvy, sexy. Bec has her shit together.

Becca: Sweet and gentle, my arse. Becca has the IQ of one of the heads of the Manhattan Project, the determination of a one ton white pointer that's doing 50km/hr right behind you, and an overall understanding of 'the bigger picture' that the Archbishop of Sydney would pay alot of money for.

Beige: Brazenly tough, while at the same time delicate and complex, Beige has a wise head and a composure that is far beyond her years. Thank Christ her parents never called her Stardust.

Bek: Bek loves being just that little bit different, but that doesn't detract from the notion that she is diabolically tremendous.

Bel: See Bell.

Belinda: Belinda is well groomed (or at least she tries to be), she is curvaceous and she is simple at her core.

Bell: A sleek and sexy game boat that is worth about $3 million. She can punch through most weather with ease and she spends each fishing season cruising the blue waters off Lizard Island. Not only is she fast, beautiful to look at and charismatic to be near, she's extremely determined.

Bella: Like the 3rd of 4th sequel to a popular movie, she's nice enough, funny enough, smart enough and sexy too, but original? You tell me.

Bellamy: A remarkable firestorm. As a pure observer, her exuberance borders on pomposity except that she is maximally caring and true to the core.

Belle: Where do you start? Belle is sweet and smooth and smart and pure (kind of) and sexy and knowing and loving and funny and shit-stirring. And there's more...

Bern: If you imagine Bernadette as some kind of normal person living some kind of normal, quiet life, then Bern is the figure that emerges from the nearest mop cupboard after the former has heard of some calamitous world event where people are in desperate need of a ravishing, multi-coloured super hero, and who drives all men berserk. Nice work Bern.

Bernadette: Dots of freckles cover her face and body and she occasionally gets lost. She is, however, exceptionally bright.

♀ FEMALE

Bernie: Bernie drives a truck, or at least she did in a past life. She has a great laugh and she's a good drinker.

Beryl: Beryl is a happy to get her hands dirty for the sake of the farm, her children and for the local community. And that's more than many people do in a lifetime.

Besa: Like a beautiful old motorbike with only one cylinder, she takes ages to get going (or relax) but once she does (or is) then she is arguably one of the loveliest ladies in a room. It just takes a while to get there, that's all.

Bessie: The Farmer's Truck.

Beth: Beth is a type of incense that aids one to become a soft and gentle artist. A drop of Deb would make her famous because Beth is often either a little fed-up, or she lacks the motivation.

Bethany: Nurturing. Her name sounds like good and dutiful dairy cow lumbering its way along its habitual track toward the organic dairy farmer's shed at five in the morning. But, there is far more to her than that. Far more indeed.

Bettina: Bettina is cold and complex, and not even that cold, really. She is, however, super intelligent and extremely driven.

Betty: Broccoli.

Bev: Bev makes the sandwiches for the shearers in the shed where Ruth reigns supreme. They appreciate the food and Bev's sense of humour as much as she appreciates them for doing a good job on all of her sheep.

Beverley: As the Principal of an expensive all-girl's private school, Beverley knows all the rorts because she has seen and done it all before, herself. Push her and you'll see a temper but she's nowhere near as uptight as you imagine. She's actually very generous.

Bezena: Bezena explodes into the world in the same way that Jackson Pollock threw paint at a distant canvas. Artist or not, she definitely adds colour to a scene, be it literal or metaphoric, and her occasional irrationality is something to be coveted.

Bianca: Bianca hangs out with Amber on the weekend - she'd hang out with her during the week but she's still at high school. In any case, Bianca seems so chaste and normal that most people think she is dim, but all of them are wrong.

Bibo: The brilliant. The beautiful. The becalmed. Bibo.

Billie: "Hi Billie....how is the new...??"
(the gorgeous Billie flies passed on her roller blades....)
"...So, what did you do last ni-LOOK OUT!!....."
(..Billie flies by again, narrowly missing everyone else...)
".....and what do you think of- OWW!! SHIT!!!!.."
(Billie laughs and that's all we hear before she disappears, once more, into the sunset....)

Bindi: See Bruno.

Blair: Tough on the surface, sensitive in the middle, Blair does what it takes and in a quietly determined way, even though her methods may be quite unorthodox and her dreams seemingly unrealistic.

♀ FEMALE

Blaise: Her red hair and her accent are nearly always a given but she has spark, spunk and style.

Blanche: Blanche lives with her dripping jewellery at a sea-side mansion at one of the 'finer' locales inside Sydney harbour, and she's gruff and arrogant like that old troll that lives under the bridge and eats children.

Blythe: John Wayne, eat your heart out.

Bobbie: She can't escape a maleness, and it compels her to live a bit harder than the next girl. Bobbie will therefore try most things and snub her nose at the world if people don't like it.

Bonnie: Fruity and freckly, Bonnie lassoes calves at rodeos from the saddle of a galloping horse, and she wins prizes for it.

Bourby: Independent and philosophical, Bourby plods along like a gently plodding camel. Bourby is lovely.

Bree: A rare and ornately coloured little bird with a shrill mating-call. Unsighted in the winter months.

Brenda: <u>The Queen of Dysfunction.</u>
(eg. You're sitting there watching the news when you hear a noise in the next room, but you dismiss it until the strange crackling gets louder. Suddenly you remember, and run to the kitchen where you discover that the damp phone bill that you put on the fry pan to dry-out has caught on fire and, though you don't know it yet, the entire house is about to burn down. Ironic, isn't it? That the house burnt down because of an overdue phone bill? Anyway, life goes on, your name is Brenda and this sort of thing happens all the time. But you're good fun and, generally, you have red hair.)

Brexxy: Sexy Brexxy. Her name looks and sounds like an out-of-whack spine being realigned. She's compassionate, she's holistically educated and, as one of the world's great chiropractors, she can massage even the most stressed person into a blissful boneless chicken, no worries.

Brianna: Brianna is a vivacious girl who hangs around with Alecia, Georgia, Bianca and Maya. She goes out with a boy called Dylan, Hudson or Gabriel, maybe Tom if she is feeling a bit traditional (Ryan if she was feeling rebellious) and one day she hopes that a boy with super-rich parents will arrive on the scene and sweep her away from her pseudo career, which she was never really into that much, anyway.

Bridie: A cross between a white dove and a virginal bride, Bridie is a modern-day Mother Teresa.

Bridget: Her name cuts itself off like few others and, consequently, Bridget gets flustered over every single thing, occasionally fretting badly. But, she's great to tell your problems to because she's probably experienced most of them herself, either in real life or theoretically.

Briony: The name of the supreme mystical goddess, and who you will often see depicted on a box of Tarot cards. She can see the past, she can see the future, and she is so ethereally magical that you will scarcely believe such a human being can actually exist.

Brittany: Brittany is the name given to the physical act of standing up quickly and cracking your head on the corner of something sharp that you forgot was there.

♀ FEMALE

Bron: A sexy woman with a deep voice, possibly the deepest.

Bronte: Bronte has beautiful clean lines. She might be a little slow to catch on but she's incredible when she does.

Bronwyn: Her hair is normally long and a luscious deep red in colour, but don't be fooled by the cool façade. For a hobby she organises get-togethers with her girlfriends, many of whom she can't really stomach for too long, which is why she experiences the odd petty social drama, but Bronwyn is looking for love and comfort like the rest of us.

Brook: The Female Gladiator who is prepared to takes steroids.

Brooke: The Female Gladiator.

Bryonie: Like the mood you're in after a day at the beach with salt on your skin, Bryonie is wistfully relaxed and she always seems to have plenty of time.

Caitlin: The head on train crash waiting to happen. So get out of the way...get out of here as fast you can. I mean, leave. Run. Go. Right now! GO!!.....*NOW!!!*

Calina: Her parents are Kelvin and Eileen so, thankfully, she was never going to be dull. And so it is.

Callee: A brand new silver Toyota Camry.

Cameron: A powerful Tom Boy in a fast moving world.

Camilla: The great pink hog. She loves wallowing in filth and the fact that the swill trough is all hers. Go you good thing!

FEMALE ♀

Camille: Can a person be too selfless? The answer is no, for Camille is a miracle.

Candice: One the most ambitious and competitive people in the Kingdom. Like marzipan, you either love her or hate her but she's definitely very rich, and perhaps too rich for many. (It's a personal-taste thing on our behalf and a self-obsessed thing, on hers.)

Caprice: Caprice rhymes with "Just past the point of most beautiful."
It is also the word uttered as a groan by men of every age – apart from all Tristans, naturally – at the moment when their orgasm becomes inevitable.

Cara: The Cara Manoeuvre exists for less than a second and is employed by two cowboys when they stand in the street facing each other. Some you win and some you lose, but if you lose you die.

Carine: See Karine, unless she has an accent, in which case she is probably French or Belgian, and damn-near perfect.

Carissa: Her parents hail from a beach in Greece, and this has produced a startling dark-haired woman who is feisty, intelligent and loving of only those people who have earned it.

Carla: The name of type of kiss during which both parties can't actually stop....

Carley: See Carli, basically, except that her dealings in life are not quite as smooth.

♀ **FEMALE**

Carmen: Originally from Malta, she will ask you if you want to use the bathroom even before you step into her house. I have no idea why.

Carmel: A dysfunctional woman that lives in the rich and leafy streets of Toorak, Melbourne. In a strange twist of irony, she is actually a kind soul but her good deeds are completely misread by many as being arrogant displays of ostentation. She doesn't really care about the money and, like billions of people all over the world, all she really wants is some genuine friends to love, and who love her back.

Carli: Carli has the power and confidence to go it alone. While not a dedicated troublemaker, she has the capacity to attract unwanted attention that she may not be able to shed as easily as her two sisters.

Carly: The 'y' rounds her off to perfection such that she is blessed with one of the largest and most luscious smiles in the Kingdom, and many men find her completely intoxicating as a result.

Carol: The peace-loving and well-natured Loggerhead Turtle. Despite a deep-seated desire to 'break out', she swims thousands of miles every year in the course of mating and giving birth, but the effort of dodging Tiger Sharks and laying countless eggs has taken its toll. She's looking forward to the next life and she deserves a break. Carol is lovely.

Carolina: The name of a Spanish dance that is complicated, passionate and energetic. Get it wrong and you'll look like an A-Grade fool, but get it right – and you'll have to dedicate yourself – then the rewards are endless. Good luck!

Caroline: A powerful and sexy 'chick', who runs her own arms company and who never makes the same mistake twice. She lives in Geneva, Switzerland, and is now worth millions.

Carolyn: Carolyn is rather refined, either in real life or in her own head, and she would rather die than flash her breasts in any kind of public space.

Carrie: Carrie is extremely beautiful but she killed her parents when she was very young because she discovered that they'd lied to her about the milk being low fat. It was full cream.

Casey: As a passionate and intense soul, Casey gets bored at the drop of a hat. She is quite sexy on her day and while no one knows what she does for a living, she's definitely not a knitter.

Casey-Lee: Apprentice beautician.

Cass: Very driven, highly intelligent, and with a knowledge of Australian foreign affairs that is second to none, Cass is a highly regarded ASIO operative and one of the groups most skilled interrogators.

Cassandra: Cassandra rides a big white horse on a beach in the nude, in slow motion, but 'Cassandra' is also the name given to the sound of any long hair that swooshes.

Cassie: The Realist. She can't be badgered into doing anything.

Cat: All boys are desperate to know her. She exudes.......
something incredible.

♀ FEMALE

Catherine: A normal smooth-skinned, fast swimming, elegant cetacean that wanna-be hippies hang posters of, on the wall. Yes, dolphins are very smart, very successful, they form complex social groups, have a highly developed language, look good.....etc, etc, etc.

Catriona: Why, Catriona is a Rosella parrot in full plumage, darling.

Caz: Another of the Gifted Ones. This girl is relaxed in her life, funny in company, intelligent if she feels like speaking, incredibly beautiful without flaunting it and more adaptable to hardship than most. There's no question to be had: Caz is someone worth knowing and loving from any angle.

Cecilia: You have to stutter in order to say her name and Cecilia therefore stutters through life, completely altering her desires and her perceived path in the universe as frequently as the weather changes. She's good fun though.

Celeste: A sexy girl that enjoys her stargazing so much she's developed a bruised chin from walking into things with her head in the air.

Chantal: Chantal has a stronger self-belief than her sister, below, and she couldn't care less if people deem her to be proud and loud in the way she operates. She would have made an excellent hunting eagle.

Chantelle: Strong self-belief. Chantelle is into real estate and the markets so it makes sense that, despite her rather quiet nature, she is quite competitive.

Charity: Rare, beautiful and pure like bush honey, Charity does just about anything she wants and with an air of nonchalance. In fact she reminds me of a recipe – has anyone tried honey-roasted potatoes lately?

Charlie: Charlie bawls her eyes out one minute and is the picture of perfect calm and confidence, the next. She'll often insist on driving herself home from the nightclub at four in the morning when she's so out of it she can hardly stand. The funny thing is that under these conditions she's one of the world's great drivers. Weird, huh.

Charlotte: Blessed with incredible luck, both perfect and farcical, Charlotte is a gifted lover, sister and partier, who enjoys nothing more than sitting around at an outdoor restaurant with her multitude of friends, while they feast on good food and wine in the summer sun. Outstanding performance, Miss Charlotte.

Charmaine: As a giraffe that strolls the African savannah, Charmaine is a long and elegant name for a slender and damn-near elegant woman. She looks down on the myriad of creatures that live in her world with a sense of fascination and wonder, engaging all those in her midst without rancour.

Chelsie: The Black Panther with a glistening coat. She's bloody dangerous when kept in the house but perfect in the wild. Please don't ever put her in a zoo.

Cherie: Piquant.

Cheryl: Cheryl works her fingers to the bone for little or no reward.

Cheyenne: Cheyenne is a complicated lass who promises much but she will have to ensure she never becomes complacent or too lazy, otherwise there is a risk she'll end up going nowhere in a hurry. Greatness is there for the taking, no question, and she can spit and curse as much as she likes, but only she can go and get it.

Chian: Deceptively normal. (Dad: Chito. Mum: Andrea)

China: The talented and solo artist, China has a tempest-like temperament.

Chloe: Chloe is a tan coloured calf that gulps down milk faster than her mum can make it.

Chris: If she'd become a rugby league cheerleader, an interior designer or an inventor, she might have become more exciting. I'm not sure. As it is, she works for the council in designing where new street lights are going to go, and she's highly skilled at it.

Chrislyn: Her name sounds like an Olympic hurdler crashing into the first hurdle and landing, splat, on the gravel. But, as long as she isn't grizzlin' Chrislyn is ambitious and excitable.

Chrissie: This girl is outrageous fun. Her only hiccup arises when she endeavours to complicate matters.

Chrissy: See Chrissie, except that Chrissy has had a child or two or three and has long since left the occasionally crazy world of 'Chrissie' behind her.

Christian: Christian is an unusual and sexual entity. She knows she has a presence and she just likes to make sure, occasionally, that you know, too. And that's okay.

Christie-Jo: Christie-Jo works in a sausage factory.

Christina: An Italian Goddess who is brown from years in the sun, and whose green eyes take you somewhere else when you look into them. She's a demon on a scooter.

Christine: Christine is intelligent and a borderline intellectual. She should have been an author rather the hard-arse CEO that she became, and she detests being called Chris.

Cinderella: Cinderella is so incredible that the only way to describe her properly is with the use of mathematics: If there are around 7.5 billion people on the planet, give or take, and there are only about 9 Cinderellas in existence, that means that she is not just one in a million, but more like one in eight hundred and thirty three million, three hundred and thirty three thousand, three hundred and thirty three point three, recurring. How good is that?

Cissy: See Sissy.

CJ: Perfectly gorgeous. Reasonably impossible.

Clair: See Claire.

Claire: A type of perfume that is packaged in the most inviting and seductive bottle imaginable, and whose initial smell is so good that it is almost overpowering. However, the chemical composition of the essence alters over time such that if too much is applied, by morning the intoxicating aroma is transformed into an unpleasant whiff that requires a good long shower to remove. (Like everything in life, moderation is the key.)

♀ FEMALE

Clara: The name of an old Massey Ferguson tractor. She loves the mud and she's super reliable.

Clare: A dedicated environmentalist and artist. Clare is so passionate about her various pursuits that she sometimes forgets to stop and smell the roses because life for her is generally wonderful.

Claudia: Claudia works for the communist party and she doesn't shower very often. She has wild black hair that befits her ardently held opinions and she becomes irate if you don't agree with her.

Cleo: As a highly intelligent Golden Retriever dog, Cleo is arguably one of the gentlest individuals on earth.

Clio: See Cleo.

Cloe: See Chloe.

Coco: The name of a plush white fur wrap-around or scarf that is draped over the shoulders of a high class hooker and, who, in turn, is tanned, curved, drop-dead gorgeous and wearing nothing else but a seductive smile.

Colette: Colette has long erratic hair and spends each morning with her head in her hands, wishing she hadn't drunk so much and smoked so many fags the night before.

Colleen: Another name that is impossible to say without wincing like you've just jammed a splinter beneath your fingernail. Is this why Colleen can be so ghastly?

Corindi: Raised with pindan between her toes and her parents' 4WD out the front, Corindi is into mud-crabbing, fishing and fighting.

Corioli: She was always going to end up near coral reefs and so she has, for Corioli is an underwater archaeologist, remembering that those that live and meditate above and below the surface of the sea tend to be strange and gifted creatures.

Cornelia: The name given to a big family pack of biscuits. Grandkids love 'em.

Corolla: $\sum \{A \text{ rather lovely and exquisite}\} + \{\text{scientist}\} \approx \infty$

Cosima: Cosima never gets embarrassed about anything, and she blasts her way through life like an unsmooth bowling ball crashing through a set of nine pins.

Courtney: If there is something that needs to be done, or some obstacle that needs to be removed, count on Courtney to take care of it. If her and Angus were together and didn't kill each other they'd move mountains.

Crystal: The middle-aged alcoholic. She's never seen without a drink in her hand and two tonnes of make-up on her face.

Cynthia: Cynthia spends more money on medicines than anyone. She's a lean woman with chronic health problems that have their root in her levels of stress. Maybe it's her lot but she's actually a very caring soul.

♀ FEMALE

Daisy: Don't be fooled by the gentle nature of her name. Beautiful, yes, sensitive, yes, but Daisy is potent as well. You bet.

Dale: A nice lady with a wonderful intent who, when she gets on in years, unwittingly leaves strange parcels of gifts on the doorsteps of all of her neighbours. They will contain things like lollies, rotting onions, scissors, old jars of relish, half-filled boxes of white wine and if you're really lucky, an old painting and maybe even a pair of underpants.

Dallas: Part tomboy, part supermodel.

Darnae: Darnae is as beautiful on the inside as she is on the outside.

Dana: Rides a Harley Davidson, has short dark hair, and absolutely adores women with a nice bum and a short skirt.

Daniella: Daniella rhymes with Mecca, and for most men, at least, she exists only as a distant image. In life she may be accustomed to a certain amount of latitude but there is no denying her rather dramatic presence.

Danielle: The name of a Grand piano whose owner insists she gets tuned, cleaned and dusted every Monday afternoon. It actually drives her bananas because all she wants to do is relax and play wonderful music, which might explain why she has such a horrible temper.

Danique: Somewhere between a perfect technique that results in unimaginably grandiose outcomes with a minimal of effort, and a full knee reconstruction that most gun-netballers experience at some point in their lives, Danique exists as a tantalising example of what might be possible. It is therefore a given that she is slightly eccentric.

Danni: Danni is a gifted genius that no-one understands and she is always just a little bit lost. She cops a lot for her beliefs and if she wasn't such a decent person, deep down, she would have made a great spy.

Darcy: Darcy has a dimpled smile and is occasionally extremely sarcastic. As a sensual being from millions of years ago, she's an intense girl that generally gets what she wants.

Daria: Diligent and busy, Daria possesses an excellent work ethic.

Darian: There's a good chance that she is quite domineering – especially if she's South African – but Darian's great quality is that she speaks only the truth, whether it hurts for someone to hear it or not.

Davina: Beautiful, exotically charismatic and temperamental, Davina is the chief curator for most of our best art galleries.

Dawn: Her name sounds like a rubber gum boot being extracted from a pond of mud, but she's far sweeter and savvier that that. Yes, Dawn is understated, but beneath her skin is a beautiful and generous soul and on her day she is fucking hilarious.

Deb: Welcome to a wonderful and unsung Enigma. The length of her name is exactly inversely proportional to her level of charisma, sexiness, directness and her capacity to get the job done. Deb is a marvel.

Debbie: A tough hombre in all situations, she overcomes hurdles in an instant with a smile and a huff of having to deal with the occasional idiot, and she's far sexier than she sounds.

♀ FEMALE

Deborah: The Perfectionist. Deborah has a wardrobe full of cashmere sweaters and plans everything to the exact last second such that she's arguably the most punctual of any creature in the animal kingdom.

Debra: Debra doesn't piss-fart around. Sure, she's got style and brains and a sense of humour, and she's sexier than even *she* possibly realizes, but her great skill is forcing others to get their shit together.
(Note: It is a given that hers already is, unless she flies off the handle, in which case disregard the entire paragraph.)

Dee: Dee has 11 children and lives a busy life. Flustered by very little, as a younger woman she was drop-dead gorgeous.

Deidre: Proper, funny and true.

Delta: Perfectly shaped with a mystical kind of presence, but something about her is upside down...

Demi: Demi is about 4 inches tall and wears a tiny little tutu. She plays the flute and flies around the sky using her dragonfly wings, while at the same time casting spells on people that force them to smile giddily, and dream of lemonade and/or fornicating in fields.

Denise: Denise has been through three divorces and is tired of bullshit, although she hasn't lost her sense of humour. She is now more comfortable in her skin than she's ever been.

Denita: Idealistic. If she isn't a full-blown political animal, then Denita is intimately involved with issues regarding personal or human rights within society.

Di: A cool cat. She has short dusty blonde hair, she can light a campfire, take a funny restaurant order and she can organize 100 kids at once. Yep, Di is excellent value. Did I say she was sexy?

Diana: She left half an hour ago and didn't say where she was going. I don't know when she'll be back. Let me know if you hear from her.

Diane: Diane is the name of a legal contract drawn up by expensive lawyers – corporate or otherwise – that has 3 minutes of glory before being filed away in the drawer forever.

Dillie: English-Frumpy-English.

Djana: Djana wears matching jewellery and is eager to impress people. She possesses a stylish walk and somehow manages to stand casually with her legs crossed.

Dolly: Big boobs, maybe, but there is more to her than that. To cope with this nickname – if it's a nickname – requires a personality with spunk, intelligence and an unselfconscious sense of fun. (N o t e : Normal-sized or small-breasted Dollys are often even funnier and more intriguing, only because they aren't compelled to surrender to their title.)

Dolores: What a woman. She's helped so many men and women that needed a little bit of love or money that it isn't funny.

Dominique: A double agent who has a foot in the KGB. She'll do what she needs to do without fear nor favour. She's as sexy as hell and it makes her job a lot easier.

♀ FEMALE

Donna: Somewhere in her heritage is a struggling mum living in a humpy, but not anymore. Today, Donna is an adaptable and pro-active whip-cracker who thinks it all, does it all and laughs heaps amid the cacophony of modern life. Madame, take a bow.

Doreen: The great and sacred cow. She lives in the fields of India, not far from the River Ganges, and munches thick lush grass, all day long, disbelieving of how perfect each one of them is.

Doris: Who knows what she looks like but she's a great comedienne. Sexy or not, she attracts more weirdos than anyone else in the kingdom and, consequently, she needs to carry a gun.

Dorota: Dorota has her standards and she will only cross those boundaries if and when she is sure the time is right.

Dorothy: Dorothy is a fence paling that's fallen off due to the nails rusting out completely and she now lies on the back lawn that has grown so tall around her that you can barely see her. Poor Dorothy, you might say, but beneath her is a teeming metropolis of snails, worms, bugs and beetles that she lovingly tends. She's been nominated for this year's Nobel Peace Prize and let's hope she wins it – she deserves it.

Dot: Mrs. R.M. Pragmatic.

Drew: Beware the Sleeping Dragon. I'll say that again.... BEWARE THE SLEEPING DRAGON!

Dug: See Duglass.

Duglass: A woman cannot be called Dug, or Duglass, unless she is in the Top 10 most charismatic, outgoing and love-generating people on the planet. Please utter a small prayer of thanks if you hear that one exists. Bless you.

Dusty: Dusty is nearly always a blonde, but she is definitely a Top 5 Enigma. Not just because of the rarity of her existence, but because the power, spunk and savvy coolness of this goddess is inversely proportional to her number in the wild. So, never try and put her in a cage and get as many photographs of her as you can, although like Duglass above her, you'll be lucky if you even see one.

Dyna: Dyna is so relaxed in life that she can sleep anywhere. It's a great skill and she'd make a great long-distance space traveller, not only because she can put herself into a coma without too much preparation, because apart from being a gifted lateral thinker, her calm and understanding nature means that she is good company for any amount of time.

Dzenita: Precocious in youth, lazy in adulthood.

Dzifa: A brand of soluble aspro.

Eadie: The Gorgeous Powerhouse.

Ebbeny: Ebbeny places a high priority on wearing the right clothes and living in the right house that's in the right suburb. With regard to her occupation, she'll look for something in the lower echelons of the legal system, a swank accountancy firm or, in a more outgoing specimen, perhaps something in the TV game.

Ebony: A professional hockey player whose competitive nature made her lethal. Sadly, the name was too energetic for any middle aged human body to handle and Ebony died young. Luckily, however, she was reincarnated as a Piranha Fish and now lives in the Amazon Basin of North Central Brazil. Life's a beach.

♀ FEMALE

Eddie: The optimistic and sensual risk-taker.

Edith: Edith has led a long and happy life. Kids, grandkids, travel, turmoil and euphoria - you name it, she's done it. What a gal.

Edwina: Edwina is a survivor and a woman of substance.

Eileen: Swears like a trooper, brews her own beer and fishes for Barramundi professionally.

Elaine: "Will I wear this blouse? Maybe that one? What about this skirt? Will that blouse match this skirt? Or what about *that* one? Is Arthur going to be there? Hang on, I better try something else....what about *this* one?"...... and so on, and so on.

Eleanor: Regal. There is 71% probability that Eleanor is incredibly boring, which is okay when you consider that she is one of the first people to act when a situation becomes life threatening.

Elise: Shy like grass. Why is that? Elise is absolutely stunning, normally, and she drives a low riding sports car that says all that she doesn't.

Elizabeth: Elizabeth owns an opulent dining room full of fine china and heavy silver cutlery. Her grand house has an Aston Martin parked out the front, and she has had a crush on the right side of Julio Iglesias's head since she was a little girl.

Elka: A cross between a cute little Eskimo man wearing deer fur and Bambi, the baby deer, Elka exists as the perfect circle of life. Sexy as hell with a clean view of the world, and of herself, Elka milks the moments for their worth with the luxury of someone who embodies the big picture as well.

Ella: Ella rhymes with, "Yeah...whaddaya want?"
And it takes a lot of energy for her just to say it, let alone act on the answer, which she will if she thinks she needs to.

Ellen: Ellen frowns constantly, even when she's happy.

Ellie: The sensual female monk. Not much really seems to faze her because she believes that everything in the world is linked, and that all things are part of an ever-changing system of energetic flux. In a nutshell, she is optimistic, young at heart, and she knows that good things come, and good things go.

Elly: See Ellie.

Elvira: A drop-dead raven-haired fire-ball who is deliciously naughty and/or evil.

Em: An affable, funny and sexy doer who means well and does well.

Emily: Appreciated by all Elizabeths everywhere, Emily is the current Table Manners World Champion. She won it in Zurich three months ago and Daylight was second.

Emma: Like the surface of a swollen river after the monsoon, she's smooth and bubbling on the surface, but all those m's are almost too perfect to be true because beneath them is a chaotic riverbed of drama and complexity. Befriend one and you must ask yourself the question: Can I swim?

Emmy: Chatterbox.

♀ FEMALE

Emmylou: Emmylou is an idiot at heart who embraces all debauched behaviour and she loves the sound of her own shrill attempts at opera singing which, sadly, are truly crap.

Enid: Enid is the name of any grandmother that interrupts a game of backyard cricket with a tray of ANZAC biscuits and raspberry cordial, although she always did like beautiful young boys.

Erica: Illogical. Neurotic. Schizophrenic. Although, perhaps it's not all her fault because Erica is occasionally infected by mean-spirited ghosts that make her behave very erratically, sometimes dangerously.

Erin: Erin is relaxed, sensual, playful and, despite her occasionally serious look, she rarely loses her sense of humour. She keeps fit, physically and spiritually, and she does it all amid a whirlwind of friends and socialness because she lives her life for her and not for anyone else.

Eske: She's Dutch, and so she knows what an esky is, already. That is, a venue for fun and friends. And so she is.

Esme: Nah, forget the hype. Esme is lovely, downright lovely. Indeed, everyone, stand to attention and salute. Thankyou. Thankyou Esme.

Estelle: This girl has a smile that's wider than the horizon and a laugh that can be heard for miles, and the ghosts of her ancestors tread the Australian landscape, still.

Esther: If Esther isn't in a nursing home, then she is young, incredibly intelligent, wears comfortable shoes and cackles loudly. Like a few others in the Kingdom, however, the energy she generates also gives her the capacity to attract weirdos by the 100's.

Ethel: Good old fashion shoe polish. Big in the 50's.

Eunice: A cross between Janice and a lump of wood, as a very expensive life-like doll made in Japan for extremely lonely men, Eunice looks incredible but there is some question as to whether or not she is plugged in. Anyone got a double adaptor?

Ev: Ev is everyone's great mate because everyone feels comfortable around her. (Unless, of course, you happen to be one of the few people that she detests, and you would need to be a complete prick/bitch to achieve that.)

Eva: Powerful and sexy when she needs to be, Eva is forgiving, compassionate and deliciously unselfconscious, everywhere else. Like Estelle above her, she laughs with her whole body and it affects all those within earshot. There was never any doubt; Eva is an incredible woman.

Evangelina: The name of a seldom-heard-of play by William Shakespeare. Basically, it's a story of a beautiful young peasant girl, the young man who loves her, and the effect she has on the King (and monarchy) after a chance encounter by the main castle gates, one day. In short, it's an explosive tale of love, ambition and betrayal that will remain with you long after you leave the theatre.

Eve: Eve often stands with her head slightly tilted, and with a look on her face that resembles melancholy leaves falling from a tree at the end of autumn. She's a lovely girl but why is she always the bearer of bad news? ....I don't get it.

Evelyn: The sweet-smelling, ever-loving tourniquet.

♀ FEMALE

Evizel: Evizel is complicated – you might as well try and explain why an Echidna tries, unsuccessfully, to dig its way into a pile of gravel – but the important thing to remember is that Evizel rhymes with Everythingsgonnabealrightintheend. And it is.

Evy: What a woman? She's cares about you and the world, she listens, she gives good advice and she laughs all the time. In fact, where is she when you need her?

Fabienne: *(Said with a heavy French accent.)*
Bonjour my darling-eh, she is, how you say...very beautiful, no?
She does not work....but....I think....ahhh, so what? Why should she? I mean....what would she do? (Hands tossed in the air, unknowingly.)

Faith: Faith lives for Friday night bingo.

Farah: Her bathroom is full of coastal themes that highlight what might have been had tragedy not struck as often as it did. Outside the bathroom she struggles, although she does look wonderful in the shower.

Fatima: Fatima is a loud and generous lover.

Fay: (Sung to any decent rap melody)
My name is Fay
If you don't get out of my way
You're gonna' suffer
Great dismay.

Felicity: The Stalker. Felicity can be very sexy but she's definitely quite crazy.

Fi: "Get out of my way!" she barks, heading for the bar/party/car keys/front of the queue/cupboard/fridge/bedroom/spa/diving platform/dance floor/anything.

Fiona: There are no in-betweens with Fiona. Either she's plain and a bit dull, or she is incredibly sexy, ambitious, charismatic and occasionally stressed. Regardless of which one she is, however, Fiona would go to the hairdresser every day if she could. Outside her bad hair days – of which there are at least five every week – she's surprisingly chilled out.

Fish: Possibly Swiss, Fish is clean living and clean thinking, if not on the surface then definitely at her core. And, naturally, she's great in, on and under the water.

Fitzy: Frisky. Despite her bull-approach in the professional arena Fitzy is a surprisingly sensitive soul. Like trillions of beings throughout the universe, all she really wants to do is hang out with the one she loves, meet with her friends, and contemplate what she might get up to tomorrow. Is that so much to ask?

Fleur: It's not possible for anyone to be as soft and as perfect as the sound of her name, and so it is. Fleur might be the first drops of rain from the storm, she might be the wayward personality with delusions of grandeur, and she might be the hard-hitting journo'. Who knows? This girl is anything but normal and she does non-normalness very well.

Flick: The sensuous and intelligent blonde who is rollicking good fun. Like any half-decent Bower Bird, she is attracted to all bright and shiny metal objects; bracelets, brass knuckles, 9mm nickel-plated pistols, wedding rings, stainless steel shackles, handcuffs....you name it. Friends and lovers, have you got a padlock?

♀ FEMALE

Florence: Florence is 92 yrs old and lives in a small country town in outback Australia. If everyone knew what she knew, and lived as simply as she did, peace on Earth would become a rapid and remarkable reality.

Foxy: She almost gives Lainey a run for her money in terms of a laid-back nature, but Foxy has that spark of charisma that allows her to pack a punch. And yes, she's a wonderful flirt.

Fran: Often caught in the mire of life's chores, she's a more generous person than most. Aside from being gifted with special psychic powers did you know that in her cupboard are heaps of sexy suspenders?

Frances: Frances enjoys wearing big black boots with steel caps. She clomps around the house making lots of noise, which makes up for her quiet nature, unless she's hungry of course, in which case she clomps loudly and with genuine purpose.

Francesca: A wonderful woman who is full of life, love, compassion and humour. She has more complications during her pregnancy and subsequent labour than any other woman, however, and if she can survive all of those then she'll have a big and wonderful family. We wish her well.

Freya: Freya rhymes with 'Easy does it', but she grew out of that. As a fashion designer of some note, these days she is extravagant and laid-back. Indeed, nothing isn't impossible for this persona.

Frida: Sensual and affectionate, Frida is occasionally overly sensitive.

Frog: Frog wears her name like one of those English pubs that has a name like, The Pork Horn and Miss Dingleberry's Underpants.
Lovely girl. Nice pub.

Gabby: Friendly to all, Gabby's optimism is appreciated by most people and she is envied by women for her slight figure and her talkative nature. But more significant than that, Gabby is brave.

Gabriela: Question: What does she do?
Answer: Anything she wants.
Not only because of her looks, but all doors will open for this girl because there are some people that, somehow, have been touched by magic. I don't understand it myself.

Gabrielle: Gabrielle drives men berserk by getting regularly on her motorbike while wearing a mini-skirt and, because she's a pragmatic and quirky soul, she doesn't understand their reaction at all. She has short hair.

Gai: Gai is not all that feminine and she is quite bare-knuckled about it all, but if you want to get something done in a hurry, and done properly, then you could do a lot worse than getting her on board.

Gail: Her name is as about as much fun as hacking off frost bitten toes with a knife and so Gail is naturally pretty tough, yet she's a funny and relaxed character who is good company. And she makes an excellent CEO. Not bad, eh?

♀ FEMALE

Gemma: Usually physically gorgeous, Gemma is deceptively ambitious and will use her sexy smile to help her anyway she sees fit. Life is a game for her and she therefore devotes as much time as possible to having as much fun as possible. She is a loud drunk.

Genevieve: Slender, elegant and with a glorious sense of self, this girl operates from another realm. Your head sways with the euphoric grace of a Puccini aria as you say her name ......*Genevieve.* Few may understand her properly and so what.

Genia: She's not a Jeanie, she's not a Fairy and she's no Genius. What Genia is, however, is enthusiastic and caring.

George: George does everything quite easily, and the only hiccup is that the maleness of her name blinds men to her true and natural beauty, which is both unique and substantial. So, look again gentlemen. (She'd make a great professional surfer.)

Georgia: A country in her own right and a person in her own skin. Ambitious and confident, just say yes when you think you should and she won't kill you.

Georgie: On one level, Georgie is a fuzzy little lamb who is so neat, cute and wonderful that she makes you want to throw up but, thankfully, no one is that nice and she taps into this empathy to go a long way.

Georgina: Aren't female chimps terrific creatures? When Georgina is in heat, her hind-quarters become red and swollen but you'd be a fool to assume that she wasn't outstanding value and highly intelligent. Absolutely.

Geraldine: The beautiful old girl became extinct about 65 million years ago when a meteor struck the earth somewhere near where Mexico is today. Prior to her extinction she was a giant herbivore that left piles of dung that were larger than a small car. What a wonderfully happy soul she was.

Germaine: In a past life her name was Len.

Gerry: Gerry is a scrumptious handful.

Giaan: A cocky male rooster trapped in a female body.

Gib: "Just give it here..!" she whines at her stage manager. She takes the ream of paper in her hands and studies it intensely. She frowns for a few seconds, flips over a page, then another, and then shoves it back in his face. "...Nup. Piece of piss," she says. "Relax. Now fuck off while I get changed."
Gib.

Gilda: Say her name once and it stops and starts and falters, say it three times and you see the truth because it was there the whole time; that is, she might not be gilded in the classical sense but she's certainly one of the great German secrets. Gilda is unusual and utterly lovely.

Gill: Her name is impossible to say if you're anywhere near sleep and thus she carries a big, sexy, brash personality. She loves mingling with different people, the more the merrier, and she loves a good game of hide-and-seek.

Gillian: The tall and intelligent psychology student who wears vivid red lipstick and the brightest dresses anyone has ever seen. (They're often covered with big embroidered flowers.) Anyway, she's raucous fun and a nightmare to argue with.

♀ FEMALE

Gina: Option A: Sexy without being sensual. Passionate without being focussed. Unstable without being dangerous.

Option B: The name of Kirsty's vagina.

Ginger: A sexy box of fizz and fun and honesty and light!!

Gisele: The sensuous heart breaker.

Giz: Giz fights for the cause for which she quite happily forgoes any kind of ego or self-promotion, and so she doesn't really look normal, either, thank Christ.

Gladys: Forget the boring social morays. Regardless of her socioeconomic status, if Gladys is at a party and, out of the blue, someone asks her to open her mouth and stick her tongue out in order to have her picture taken, she will immediately agree with unadulterated enthusiasm. The world needs more of them.

Glenda: Glenda is a peach that is devoid of any momentum. She was perfectly ripe about four weeks back but she fell from the tree a week ago and is now lying on the ground, beneath it, as a rather juicy lump.

Glenis: A fair dinkum, u-beaut', 100% genuine Australian Gum Tree.

Glenys: See Glenis.

Gloria: A simple and happy soul who is careful with most things. She has a permed hairdo.

46

Grace: Born as a 40 year old and therefore measured and wise before her time, Grace has great faith in her friends because she often sees their future before they do. How do you top that?

Gracie: The name of a plush white rug next to a sun-filled window that you go and lie on for a lazy nap on a winter's afternoon.

Grady: Her name is so smooth and unusually cool that people have difficulty remembering it and, consequently, her life is far more complex than it need be. But, beneath these frustrating moments, she is a sensual and worldly individual.

Gretchen: As a geology PhD student, she loves all rocks (especially igneous ones), wears boots, hiking trousers and a flannel shirt that Jake would be proud of. There is also at least one crater on Mars named after her.

Gretel: A witch. And not a very nice one.

Guinevere: Like the Yeti, Santa Claus, the Tooth Fairy and Drop Bears, we *want* her to exist but she just doesn't. Does she?

Guineveve: The name given to an exotic and fiendishly confusing maze in the plush grounds of a 16th century French or Italian mansion. Courtesans of the day attempted to fornicate in them during afternoon tea parties.

Gwen: Serious. She wears her name like a Chameleon wears its colours but Gwen is cool and electric on her day, such that you might have to look and think twice about how remarkably beautiful and/or enigmatic she is. (Note: Please read this name theory again, this time beginning at the end of the first sentence.)

♀ FEMALE

Gweneth: The Controller. If you do the wrong thing she will withdraw her love. If you do the right thing she will return it.

Gypsy: Gypsy swirls though life with such chaotic magnificence that nothing ever gets done. Who knows what she does with her life, but she's certainly happy.
WARNING: Don't give her any whisky unless it's an emergency.

H: The savvy project manager. She gives a lot – maybe too much – and she has so many friends (of both sexes) that she hasn't got the time to see them all.

Hailey: Hailey is basically the same as her twin sister (Haley) although she is more daring.

Haley: As a little girl she always wanted a pony but her family could never afford one. Full of good intentions for everyone and everything, she's a good soul and good company.

Hannah: As a little girl Hannah played the violin and she was always berated by her mother for not applying herself more. Today, she is a gentle soul who is searching for the gentle rock of love.

Harriett: Harriett is full of pep and possibly even a decent sized ego, but she's an odd one. Her carefully nurtured childhood, for example, might have given her one of the sweetest voices ever created. Then again, she might have become the compassionate Head Warden of a womens' prison. Who knows?

Hazel: Hazel is at ease. Hazel is warm. Hazel is wonderful.

Heather: If Heather doesn't spend each day in bad weather, she does a special rain dance and concocts it herself, sometimes quite unconsciously.

Heidi: A German wrestler who was given her name by her manager because he insisted she do something to soften her image. And it nearly worked.

Helen: Now here is the sort of woman who gets things done but rarely receives the kudos she secretly needs or deserves. As a rather complex soul, Helen doesn't have time to try and be sexy – either she is or she isn't – for there's simply too much weight on her shoulders to worry about such banalities.

Helena: Helena is the name of the sound produced by two large, smooth chunks of limestone being rubbed together. For such a harsh activity the sound that is produced is surprisingly exotic and calming. *"Hey hey…,"* the noise will tell you, soothingly. *"…..it will be alright."* (Just be careful not to put your fingers in between them.)

Hilary: Hilary has a cut-glass English accent that matches her haughty demeanour.

Hilly: Incredibly clumsy and forgetful, Hilly's moments of greatness and great achievement arrive largely as a complete fluke. And she's chirpy.

Holly: Spurned in school by the girls for being too wonderful, she flourished in her teens when she became a model. When she tired of that she went pro with the cello and the last I heard she was about to become the Chief Researcher at the Parkes Observatory.

♀ FEMALE

Honey: Languid and delicious.

Honie: The name of any stunning Pacific Ocean tropical sunrise. That is, she is a vivid orange sun, and she is the warm still air that smells of clean ocean salt.

Hytal: A pristine waterfall in an untouched rainforest.

Imelda: Cute and mysterious, no one is sure if Imelda is the consummate actress or if this is just how she is. The only certainty is that she is affiliated with the artistic world, someway, somehow.

Imogen: Imogen has multiple orgasms nearly every day and therefore always looks like she's about to have another one. Nice work if you can get it.

Inda: Carried aloft by her seven Egyptian slaves who cater to her every whim, Inda floats around with an air of devilish intent that beguiles all those who are lucky enough to get close to her. She doesn't intend to, but somehow she manages to walk the red carpet, even when doing something as banal as brushing her teeth.

Indi: Monty Python would have loved her because her name is woody, luscious, mysterious and inviting. And so she is....

Inge: Another realist. Inge gives her all but as an older soul who knows the rules, she understands that extreme exertion, in whatever form that is, will only get her so far before the hands of luck and karma step in for the final say.

Ingrid: The plate of short bread biscuits that are slightly burnt. You look at them, expecting them to do something, but nothing happens. They just sit there.

Irene: Irene is what you say when one of the wings of the plane that you're travelling on suddenly shears off. You then yell out 'Irene' as a blood-curdling scream that lasts for two full minutes until the end.

Iris: Like a hippopotamus wallowing in a water hole, Iris is intelligent, thoughtful, utterly confident of her position in the world, and she enjoys hysterical fun only when the time is right. Then she will be *the one*.

Irma: A great Clydesdale horse that remains unbothered by any din in her midst.

Isabella: Winter time in Venice and Isabella walks through Piazza San Marco wrapped in a plush black coat, followed by the eyes of one hundred Italian men who know a gorgeous and self-confident woman when they see one. Absolutely.

Isabelle: Isabelle hates it when she walks into a room feeling happy and cool, and people look at her and say, "Oh, poor Isabelle." I don't know why they do that, although she does hang out with Eve.

Izzy: Izzy lives quite a neat little double life: As a daytime job she is one of the Army's most gifted snipers and when she's on leave she does pretty well on the stand-up comedy circuit.

Jacinta: Jacinta loves pottery class and she tries hard.

Jack: Jack is often so busy, on her way to somewhere else, that she rarely has enough time to tell you what she's up to or where she's headed. Like her sister below, however, she is outstanding value.

♀ FEMALE

Jackie: Like all Becs, Jackie doesn't fuck around and she's probably more streetwise that anyone. She never seems to have time for overly romantic exploits but she's a sexy and sensual woman, if not in body then definitely in spirit.

Jacqueline: Hardcore.

Jacqui: It almost goes without saying that Jacqui is beautiful and wild, but for fuck sake don't ever get on her bad side.

Jade: Jade kind of floats around in a daze and, like Doreen, she's disbelieving at how wonderful the universe seems to be.

Jaimie: On one level she is completely innocent. On another, she has a tattoo on her arse and wheels through life with a Samurai sword that she's spent years training with.

Jamie: Jamie is cut from the same chunk of marble as her sister (above) but she has a greater capacity to unravel in comparatively straightforward situations.

Jan: Travel agent. She can organise nine different itineraries at once while simultaneously holding two other conversations with a bunch of annoying American tourists, who aren't even purchasing any tickets to anywhere. (She knows that before they do.) But, she rarely loses her cool and on the weekend she coaches netball.

Jana: You'll need a workman's helmet if you intend to try and get close to her because Jana is a smooth concrete wall. (She once fell over on a building site and killed a guy, that's all.)

Jane: Welcome to one of the Enigmas. You might think that Jane rhymes with 'Yes, done and finished,' but you'd be wrong. The entire word curls over in your head, and in your mouth as you say it, but the secret to Jane is to understand that you don't get the full picture until the J has come right around and gone the full circle. Then you'll see her, then you'll know who she is....

Janelle: Janelle is the phenomenon of dropping a full 2 litre carton of milk onto the floor that ruptures badly, whereupon it covers the entire area in a sticky mess that takes three separate mopping events to clean up.

Janet: The tenacious ex-girl guide who actually holds a world record. At least twice every winter Janet will find herself standing on a curb on a wet day, on her way to work, when a bus suddenly appears from nowhere and crashes through a puddle of water on the road in front of her. All she has time to do is look in horror as the wall of water comes toward her, drenching her completely.

Janice: QUICK....GET AN AMBULANCE! IS SHE ALIVE? CHECK HER PULSE!

Janie: After backing your car into a telephone pole, she opens the door and hops out, shrugs her shoulders at you and smiles. "Oh well, sorry about that, but it's just a car."
And she's right — it is just a car. The strange truth of the matter is that, of all the people you'd like to crash your car, Janie is the one. She is a happy soul with a rare smile and she's therefore hard to say no to. In the annuls of the universe, therefore, you might as well give her your keys and ask her to crash it again. It'll probably be funny.

♀ FEMALE

Janine: Have no fear. Get on the phone, call the RAC and they'll come out and fix your Janine (flat tyre) right away. Call 1000 1000.

Jasmine: Despite her initial shyness, she's flourished into a sweet smelling, fast thinking, affable Goddess who turns a room when she's wearing a blue dress.

Jax: Miss W.B Sarcastic Bastard, who went to Thailand years ago and got a tattoo on the back of her neck that she was told said 'Lotus'. Turns out that it translates as 'Crack Whore', which she's obviously not.

Jayde: If Jade is a brand new ladies silver Rolex watch, then Jayde is the Indonesian imitation, and from up close you'd be hard-pressed to tell the difference.

Jayma: Jayma rhymes with "Can't someone else do it?" It therefore takes a great effort for her to achieve a great deal and she's a bit sick of feeling like she has to.

Jazz: Jasmine isn't really a follower of rules, anyway, but Jazz (and especially Jazzy, if she's around) goes out of her way to break them, or at least to see what is possible in the universe. So long as she never decides to get breast implants she'll be wonderful, even though everyone would still love her if she did.

Jean: The Ultimate Matriarch.

Jemaya: Jemaya is cute, normal and reliable, but she's about as earth-shattering as a box of Weeties, or maybe Coco Pops.

Jemima: As a gorgeous ex-North American Indian squaw, Jemima is possibly the most beautiful and charismatic Tom Boy in existence.

Jennifer: If she insists on being called Jennifer then you must say hello and, even if you don't know any martial arts, at least pretend to make some kind of karate defence stance. If she doesn't attack, make a hasty retreat. That's it.

Jenn: Sexier than she thinks or knows, Jenn enjoys people and gets on well with everyone, and she is a good friend to have – on all levels – at least 89% of the time.

Jenna: Jenna is a sexy girl, probably, but one more 'n' in her name and you would risk falling asleep shortly after you met her. As it is, you hear her name and for a moment you wonder if you misheard it; "Was that Jenn, Jemma or a kitchen mop, I just met?" In summation, Jenna is a nice person because her name leaves you with nowhere dangerous to go.

Jenni: High pitched nasal voice. Trivial concerns.

Jenny: The Community and family stalwart who is hard-working and very polite.

Jerry: Jerry fights the masculine shit in her name, head-on, by being dashing, daring and exotic.

Jessica: Frumpy. She wails at her own birthday party when she realizes that there aren't enough presents, of which there rarely is.

Jess: Jess may or may not be the most stunning girl in the room, but she certainly does nothing by halves.

Jessie: Jessie lives on a farm that's had no rain for six years and she's skilled at putting down horses with the back of an axe.

♀ FEMALE

Jesuloluwa: Her family hails from somewhere on the African continent and apart from being born with natural rhythm, all we know is that she has an amazing smile that will lead her on quite an unexpected path.

Jill: Jill is kind of fun but she's a bit too organised.

Jillian: The manager of the typing pool. She rules her girls with an iron fist, and there is a rumour going around that she might have had something to do with the disappearance of her ex-husband.
Note: There's at least some red in her hair.

Jo: Highly intelligent and extremely thoughtful, Jo is a sensitive girl. Once in a while she is reasonably psychotic but, generally, she's adaptable and compassionate.

Joan: Joan = Jennifer Hawkins + The Hulk.

Joanie: Joanie is content and bubbly in a drab-happy fashion, unless she's a Kiwi. In which case, she regularly rappels down the faces of mountain cliffs, builds houses in order to promote her empire, and divvies out goodies like they're going out of fashion. (Note: Like all Kiwis, however, as usual, she is dangerous when out of it.)

Joanna: Joanna was screamed at by her parents as a child quite a bit, so these days you can't blame her for being off in her own little world for most of the time.

Johanna: As a lioness in a past life, Johanna enjoys nothing more than lounging around the house in the nude and sleeping as much as possible. Having done all her killing eons ago, these days she's a sensitive soul with a soft name, and she is much better suited to lazy life on the French Riviera.

Joanne: Joanne rhymes with Routine.
As an accountant who lives in Mt.Isa, she made herself famous at the office last summer during that hot spell. It was 44 degrees at 2pm for two weeks straight and she wore her grey woollen skirt <u>every</u> <u>single</u> <u>day</u>.

Jocelyn: Jocelyn was reared by foster parents after her biological parents were killed in a plane crash when she was three. However, her foster mother, jealous of her intelligence and niceness, made her life a misery. She is a librarian now and, Jocelyn, it's never too late to be anything you want, so what are you waiting for?

Jocy: Jocy rhymes with Cosy, almost, and she kind of fits when you least expect it.

Jode: Feared by many and loved by many, Jode has a mean temper like her occasionally twisted sisters, below, but she's far more relaxed. She drives fast on the road and expects others to do the same, and she's extremely sexy, but not many people know that she can actually see the aura of individuals when she puts her mind to it. Jode is an incredible woman.

Jodi: See Jodie, except that she is slightly less abrasive, and slightly more illogical.

Jodie: Similar to a gorgeous looking feral cat, if you corner her or piss her off there is a fair chance you won't live to tell the tale. But, feed her well, stay out of her way if she's in a bad mood and mind what you say in her presence, and you'll be fine.

Jody: See Jodie, except that she is slightly less intelligent.

Joe: Surprisingly doleful.

♀ FEMALE

Joey: The cheeky life of a cheeky party and/or swingers' gathering.

Johnno: Men want her. Women want to be like her. She works for either an ad agency or a publishing house and she's good at what she does. Not really belonging in the fast lane, Johnno seems well-suited to a life by the beach in Sydney's eastern suburbs, or maybe on the mid-north coast.

Jonika: Jonika seems to get off on confrontations and she's definitely good to have around when difficult projects need to be finished-up.

Joscelin: See Jocelyn.

Josephina: Josephina is a border-line saint. Had Sleeping Beauty been drawn with blonde hair instead of black, this would have been her name.

Josephine: A beautiful romantic who is often let down by the men in her life. In short, she's the perfect wine glass waiting for the perfect wine.

Joss: Joss owns a pair of hiking boots that have trekked across the Andes, through Nepal, and currently are taking her up Cradle Mountain in Tasmania. She lights a mean campfire, struggles with the bullshit in the real world and almost never wears make-up, deodorant or perfume. Joss, we salute you.

Joy: An old fashion version of Ally. She loves drinking a nice whisky with her grandchildren, although her children would freak out if they ever found out.

Joyce: The Stalwart. She's past middle age nowadays and more relaxed with herself and the state of the world, but she still possesses a load of spunk. Joyce will tell you what's wrong with you without the slightest compunction and then give you a kiss on the cheek, afterwards, to remind you that she still loves you. And she does. And that's what matters.

Juanita: Juanita has the personality and demeanour of an old pot being clanged repeatedly by an enthusiastic six year old wielding a metal ladle, and who is helping his or her mother, father or guardian concoct dinner.

Jude: Jude works at the pub where she pulls a mean beer. Laughs a lot. Fights hard.

Judith: "Oh, Judith!" you cry, after the shit of a pigeon lands in your hair. Soon, though, you remember that it is good luck and you smile.

Judy: Yeah, Judy is great. Just be careful because she carries a concealed weapon most of the time. It's all good, but just be careful.

Jules: Jules is pretty cool and all you have to do is look at her close female friends to understand why; Jackie, Stef, Bec, Janie, Nat and Libs. That says it all.

Julia: Like a loud and busy kitchen after someone has just dropped a stack of plates, Julia is all over the shop.

Julie: Julie is pretty normal but once in a while, at least, Julie rhymes with Flustered, Happy and Late, and occasionally Slightly Needy.

♀ FEMALE

Juliet: Like Repunzel, Juliet sits in a locked room at the top of the castle awaiting the arrival of her knight in shining armour. Not a Richard, for he cannot see the castle today, more like a knight called Dudley. Dudley the Knight? Are you out there, boy?

June: June used to swim in the Murray River as a little girl and, now, as a mature and wise adult, she is a rock for everyone she knows and loves. To be honest, like Carol, she could probably use a few months away.

Justine: The mortar that holds any brick wall together. There's nothing flashy or incredibly sexy about Justine but try building a civilization without her.

Kahlia: Receptionist.

Kahran: Picture Karen, born of Northern European parents, like Sweden or somewhere. She is therefore slightly more aloof than normal, but rollicking and independent good fun, nonetheless.

Kahri: Kahri is a good-looking, elemental girl who seems to attract unstable men.

Kaia: Kaia is a sensual, ambitious and well-travelled woman with a healthy view of herself. As a result of spending her life having to constantly spell her name to people, she takes no shit from anyone and she doesn't tolerate fools.

Kalina: Despite having a name like the type of motorcar that could be described as a people-mover, Kalina is a good, normal person. She won't find a cure for HIV or malaria but she won't deliberately pour sugar into the fuel tank of your car in order to destroy it, either.

Kalo: (Pron. Kar-loor.) A unique name has produced a unique woman – sensuous, big personality, great singer/actor/sculptor/painter and the life of the party. If a doomsday festival is ever held in light of Earth's imminent demise, her name would be on the VIP guest list.

Kammy: The all-loving hippy mother who is rarely on time.

Karen: In a world of death, famine, war, drought, disease, suicide, mortgage payments and stubbed toes, Karen is a welcome relief because she is Ultra-Double Normal. (ie. compassionate, optimistic, occasionally very sexy and surprisingly adventurous.)

Karine: Karine, hear this: It's never over 'til it's over. Fight the tempest within! FIGHT IT, I SAY! GRIT YOUR TEETH AND FIGHT!...GODDAMN IT!!!

Karina: Karina is a perennial optimist who is sporty and outdoorsy, and competitive to boot. She's the sort of knock-about girl who, while at the same time as expanding her reputation in the scientific world, also represents Australia in netball at the Commonwealth Games.

Karla: Karla is a very expensive knife that is crafted in Germany. She's probably the sharpest thing in the world so be very careful. Wet or dry, however, she is an incredibly sexy woman.

Karma: Gentle and friendly on the outside and super-tough in the middle, Karma always gets what she wants.

Kasey: Kasey aspires to be the only female mechanic in the Ferrari Formula 1 racing team.

Kat: The genial Lab Technician.

♀ FEMALE

Kate: I'd check for rocks first, but Kate is the name of the breath you take before diving into a perfect blue sea. If it's a good day you'll see the rocks, no worries, and if it's a really good day then she'll take your breath away. No question.

Kath: Kath is one of the most down-to-earth and knockabout women in Australia but luck doesn't always run with her. The hard 'th' at the end of her name might act as some kind of blockage or crossroad, it's hard to say, but know this: she is a passionate and sensitive soul, reactive too, who only wants to see good deeds done.

Katherine: The name of a fine leather horse stirrup that is polished and taught, and ready for the day's parade.

Kathleen: The horrible screech produced when you drag your fingernails across a blackboard.

Kathryn: The pent-up worry wart.

Kathy: You know how a Valium makes you relaxed and ambivalent about everything? (They're excellent to take before a long bus trip). Anyway, the Kathy Pill works in exactly the opposite way.

Katie: Very attractive. Super competitive.

Katrina: 'Ka-treen-Na' rhymes with 'Oh-God-No'.

Kay: A paper cut. Not life threatening. No hospital required. It stings in the shower but, luckily, it heals quickly.

Kaya: Kaya is slightly off the ground like a hovercraft. Smooth in movement and sexy in flight, she pines for the day when she can relax in knowing what she wants in the world, and thereby afford herself the time and space to be bored for a moment.

Kaye: The Nurse.

Kayla: The scheming mastermind.

Kayleen: They made a TV ad about her years ago.....
"Ya canna' hand a man a granda' spanna'...."

Kazza: One of the boys.

Keeley: Dynamic, powerful and ready, Keeley ensures the pace of the race is never lost and that everybody else knows exactly where they're going and what they're supposed to be doing.

Keller: Is she a dedicated genius or is she just drifting along? She's almost incredible but.....where is the spark?

Kelli: An attractive reporter from any one of the commercial television networks. She doesn't quite understand our system of parliament, the legal world or the finer points of the financial markets but you'd never know it, and she dyes her hair strawberry blonde at least once every year.

Kellie: See Kelli.

Kelly: Kelly is physically attractive, outgoing and funny, but she is the sort of girl who, six months after the event, insists that all of her friends come around to watch her 4 hour wedding video.

Kelsie: Spicy and tasty, Kelsie is a type of sauce that performs somewhere between straight tomato sauce, HP, Worcestershire, Tobasco and Sweet Chilli. True, not many restaurants have ever heard of her, but she has a small if not very dedicated band of fans.

♀ FEMALE

Kerri: Spicy and energetic, Kerri always means well.

Kerri-Anne: A Bronze Whaler about 6 feet long. She looks amazing and, boy, can she move? But, Jesus, if her blood is up and you're in the water you need to have eyes in the back of your head.......

Kerry: Kerry is the sensation you feel in your nose, throat and chest when you begin to chew and swallow a mothball that you mistook for a large white mint.

Key: The Needle Point.

Khristie: See Kristy.

Kiara: Intense but nice; serious but not; intelligence not genius; travelled but homely; arty but sort of naive.

Kiera-Louise: KL drips with diamonds and pearls in the same way that she drips with affection and laughter, and so it makes sense that she provides the most exquisite and beautiful food of any non-practicing chef on the planet.

Kiki: Kiki is a Swedish Dolphin who is physically gorgeous beyond the description of any written words.

Kim: Kim actually holds a record in the Kingdom for possessing the greatest ratio of:
Complexity of nature
Name length
Indeed, Kim is sensual, she is worldly, she is determined and, yes, she is complex.

Kimberley: Kimberley has the I.Q of unknown proportions but that doesn't matter. In a world where looks count, she does alright. She's a lingerie model, and she's organized.

Kimmy: Flighty and superficial one day, hilarious and dangerous the next. Like Muchy, she can't sit in the one spot for more than about 10 minutes.

Kio: Is she Inuit, Russian, Greek or English? No one is certain but none of that is really relevant. Kio dives into situations and this is her special skill. That's not to say she carries no fear but she needs to test herself from time to time, which is why her hobbies/men/friends seem out of the ordinary. Life is an interesting game for Kio, and we will do well to see what she says about it.

Kiri: Kiri allows herself only so much down-time before she stands up, dusts herself off and heads stridently back out into the field with her guide book, her sample vials and her trusty sextant.

Kirsha: No woman is an island but Kirsha does alright. She studied art design at university although no one knows if she scored a job in that field or not. She's quite an intense lady…intense but nice.

Kirst: The pulsating and seductive dare-devil.

Kirsten: As one of life's great reality checks, Kirsten is the name of that irritating pebble in your shoe that is hard to find, even after you take your shoe off. Don't let her operate any kind of machinery, whatsoever, although she is great with animals. And she never gives up easily.

Kirstie: A female jockey. It took her a while to crack it in this male dominated world but she's a surprisingly determined girl. And she loves horses.

Kirsty: See Kirstie

Kitty: Kitty runs a business that sells sexual dress-up clothes for adults.

Klara: Gorgeous or otherwise, Klara is a decent person with a good heart who follows the trends.

Krisha: Loco.

Krista: Like a lone Jelly Fish pulsating its way through a clean ocean, Krista often produces a wonderfully unusual spectacle, not to mention a different perspective on life, but it takes her ages to get anything done and if she's in a bad mood when you touch her you'll wear the scars.

Kristie: An orthodox hot water bottle that is made out of blue rubber. She bubbles and squeaks if you touch her on the belly.

Kristy: If she isn't slightly dull then she is likely to be extremely energetic, in which case she is a possible lawyer, pole dancer or professional kick-boxer.

Kyeema: The warrior princess in waiting.

Kyla: Kyla kind of lies flat and keeps quiet.

Kylie: The Dignified Bogan.

Kym: Like her little sister, Kym is quick and often quite reactive, but she has a greater understanding of the consequences of her actions.

Kyria: The Sleeping Volcano.

Lainey: Giving. Wise. Laconic.

Lainie: See Lainey.

Lana: The Plain Jane that expects plenty without ever having to do much.

Lara: Option A: Lara floats around in a parallel cloud universe that, honest to God, does not exist. You'd never tell her that though and that's okay because ignorance is bliss.

Option B: The name of your favourite tracksuit pants that you put on in the middle of winter after a nice, long hot shower.

Larissa: Larissa spends thousands calling telephone astrological guides, hoping and praying that one day she'll be told that her life is, and will be, perfect. She retires to energy class once a week.

Larnie: The classic Earth God Mother. She lives in either Byron Bay or the hinterland, sleeps 15 hrs every day and eats organic everything.

Laura: Normally about 65% crazy. Not crazy enough not to be really sexy, kind of, and not intelligent enough to be boring, but she's definitely different, and potentially exotic. Does that make sense?

Laurel: The wonderful female priest.

Laurellee: The name of a movie genre. In this case, a comedic farce that takes place in the countryside and where everyone ends up married and living happily ever after.

Lauren: A luxurious destiny awaits you Lauren so go forth in the guise that you choose and *be* wonderful. And she always smells great.

♀ FEMALE

Lauri: Any time she puts up a fuss it is always a front because all she is really doing is letting you know that she is bored, and that she wants you to do something about it. And so she's always sort of funny when she starts complaining.

Laurie: Didactic.

Laurina: Laurina is remarkable – she's happy, she's sexy, she's honest, she's compassionate and she's funny. There just aren't many of them and for such a normal-sounding name this is probably the only mystery; *Why aren't there more of them?*
(Note: She is a true sexual deviant).

Layla: One of the gifted ones. Magic lies in her smile and her fingertips, which is a good thing because she rarely takes the easy option, but she is a rare creature whose ethereal beauty and sense of earthy wellness is offset perfectly by her laughter.

Leah: Highly strung.

Leane: Leane operates the betting machine at the pub. (Works with Jude.)

Leanne: See Leane.

Lechelle: Lechelle has big eyes, glossy lips and sells jewellery in a jewellery shop at hugely inflated prices.

Lee: Lee is often so energetic that if she were a metal object that you applied to the skin, you would hear a scorching sound.

Lee-anne: KFC manager.

FEMALE ♀

Leena: Passionate and unpredictable, Men often gravitate toward her for reasons that most of them would be hard-pressed to explain, themselves.

Leigh: There is a cross on the map that denotes the location of the treasure. It won't be an easy journey and not everyone will make it alive. This, as they say, is life. But, to get there as quickly as possible you'll need a Leigh to guide you as much as she can...... so, listen to what she says and goodluck!

Leila: This girl is suave, sensual and inviting like a semi-inflated li-lo made of suede leather, although there may be an unforgiving rock inside it that is only ever felt if the air pressure gets too low. (It's the niggling product of no one ever knowing how to spell her name.)

Leith: Submissive in the end.

Lella: Where'd she go? Is she sleeping again? And what's happened to the chocolate??

Leoni: The name of a Russian satellite that never worked properly anyway, but is now out of control and plummeting toward the Earth at 25,000 km/hr. All any of us can do is to cross our fingers and hope that she doesn't land anywhere near us. Good luck!

Leslie: As a woman cursed with a masculine name, she spent years visiting a psychiatrist. She went for so long that, in the end, she forgot why she decided to go in the first place. These days she's doing well. Always was, really.

Lesley: See Leslie.

♀ FEMALE

Leticia: Leticia doesn't tolerate idiots yet she manages to maintain her sensuality in all but the most stressful of situations. In short, she is a potent and sexy go-getter.

Lex: A bona fide Enigma. She undergoes constant metamorphosis and she could be anything – anything but boring, that is.

Lexy: Beautiful but dangerous. I mean, *seriously* dangerous.

Lib: The name of Libby when she is fast asleep.

Libby: Bipolar. Be careful.

Libs: Libs is great fun. She embarrasses her daughters.

Liesel: Like a slippery young seal, Liesel is happy, determined and sufficiently enthusiastic.

Liisi: The elusive and mischievous fairy princess.

Lil: It's Christmas morning, Darwin, 1974. Another house has just been blown away by a cyclone and those inside were lucky not to be blown away with it. Now that the tempest has passed, Lil emerges from the rear of the wreckage in a faded pair of trousers and a scraggy red cowboy shirt.
"....I found these in the bar fridge," she says, passing her husband a beer with the exhausted and sexy smile that got him there in the first place.

Lila: See Leila.

Lilach: Silky.

Lilian: Lilian is a species of hippie often seen romping naked through the forest. She makes lots of 'tweeting' noises in an attempt to speak to the birds and only rarely does she fail. Regardless of her ornithological pursuits she's excellent company.

Lily: A clinical psychiatrist that took up the profession in order to help explain her own fissured personality. She's a sexual dynamo.

Lina: See Leena.

Linda: A portly woman in adulthood, she often has a concerned look on her face – as if she is approaching a mountain bend in a car that's travelling far too quickly. This is a classic Linda moment.....

Lindsay: Her unusually stunning look is somehow complimented by the maleness of her name and the result is a unique and quite enigmatic woman. She's not the full Enigma but she's definitely an apprentice. If you intend to befriend her, however, you will need an atlas, a GPS and a psychic, just to see where you are really standing.

Lindy: Part delicate flower, part army lieutenant, Lindy treads a more volatile and/or precarious path than most.

Lindy-Lou: The Cabaret Singer.

Ling: Brazen and sexy, Ling loves tossing caution to the wind.

Linley: The reliable and stable white picket fence. There is very little rust on the latch of the gate and her paint job is in good condition.

♀ FEMALE

Lisa: Lisa is supremely normal and often quite beautiful but, better than that, she endeavours to allow herself the freedom of passionate reactions in her life.
(Note: Having said that, if aliens abduct the English-speaking world's most charismatic, mysterious and sensual woman as some kind of culture-enhancement project, Lisa probably won't be the one.)

Liss: Sexy Liss. Like the playful tip of a cat's tail, she is full of mischievous intrigue and naughty ideas.

Liv: Liv throws up when she get stressed so try not to get her stressed. Unfortunately she's so cool and calm on the surface that no-one knows whether she's stressed or just as chilled and wonderful as ever. Apart from that, no worries.

Livinia: Giggle-pot.

Liz: In a past life her name was Geoff.

Lizzie: Either very tall or very wide, Lizzie carries an infectious laugh that is just as grandiose as her physical and/or spiritual presence. Remember at all times, however, that she is as mad as a cut snake.

Lizzy: See Lizzie.

Ljiljiana: Ljiljiana will quite happily kill people in order to fulfil her objectives and her name is far too confused for her to worry about things like looks. She'd be great in the Mafia but perhaps she should have gotten into politics?

Loanne: Loanne is fun to take camping because she snores like a legend.

Lola: Tone deaf to the tune of 100%. That doesn't stop her singing though. She thinks the cats that howl in protest are actually singing *with* her, but you have to love her passion for the creative cause.

Loraine: Loraine works in the school tuck shop during the week and at the local footy ground on the weekend. She sells lots of pies, knows everyone, and no one feels bad or sad when they leave her company. (And she doesn't really care if people put two r's in her name, or not.)

Lorella: Lorella is a fluffy kind of bird that can't seem to remember why she is standing where she happens to be standing. But she means well, she laughs easily and overall she's splendid company.

Loretta: Loretta goes hard in the gym, just as she goes hard in life. You'd do well as her friend although she makes a diabolical enemy.

Lou: .....*mia principessa.* She is so cute and clumsy and forgetful that she breaks your heart, yet she's also quite determined.

Louise: You wince when you say her name and it's a position that is difficult to recover from. Maybe she's bitchy, maybe she isn't, but in one of the world's great dichotomies, if she isn't awkward in some regard then she actually turns out to be incredibly compassionate. Go figure.

Lu: See Lou.

Luana: Luana rhymes with I Wanna', and she does wanna', but the artistic and extravagant thread of her nature is often held back for some unknown reason. Her name is very rich and open, and perhaps it just holds too many possibilities? I'm not sure, but she'd make a fantastic mother.

♀ FEMALE

Lucia: Single handed, she's sailed across all the major oceans. She once had to climb on deck in a Force 10 gale off the Cape of Good Hope in order to mend a hatch cover that had come lose. It threatened the yacht and therefore her life, and can you believe that she did that at two in the morning?

Lucinda: A strong and unconventional girl. She's not that religious, really, but having been given the task of ringing the giant church bells, years ago, she'll never leave the faith. She loves getting picked up by the ropes on the upswing and shouting, "Praise thy bells!"

Lucy: Lucy enjoys making love outside, preferably in a public place, and she loves all danger. She used to be a skydiving instructor in the Caribbean until she was offered a job running guns into Alfred's old stomping ground. It was an offer too good to refuse.

Luda: Luda isn't really lewd and she's not an exhibitionist, per se, but if you could toss those qualities into a blender with one and a half shots of adrenalin and two shots of Jamaican Rum, you'd have an addictive cocktail called, The Luda. Two or three of those might change your life.

Luka: Luka may seem quiet and almost a little timid but fear and fret not. Beneath that almost boyish hairdo is one of the clearest and most adept minds in the entire Kingdom. She knows what she's doing and, even if she doesn't, she's having fun in a way that just seems weird to those that don't and/or can't understand her. She might even be another genius...

Lyndal: Unsubtle.

Lynette: A nice lady who is lean like a ballerina and possibly incredibly impatient (or just extremely ambitious).

Lynn: Lynn will take on a project no matter how unpopular, crazy or perilous it might seem. If she believes in it, she's in, and she's generally in it until the end.

Madeleine: A true thespian, be it on the street, in the lounge room or on the stage. She refuses to wear her hair short.

Madison: A spoilt brat if she remains a Madison. Maddy, on the other hand, is absolutely adorable.

Maddy: See Madison.

Madonna: Messy.

Maggie: The beautiful black, sweet-natured Labrador dog that slobbers over everything. She has the softest ears in the world.

Mags: Mags is no rock star, she's not a leader of society, she's not a criminal and she's neither abusive nor selfish. What she is, is friendly and funny.

Mako: Japanese. Apart from this making her a lover of fish, it also makes her very gracious.

Mandy: Full lips, empty head, and she has a crush on Darren – unless she's the Mandy that became an air hostess for Emirates, in which case she's brilliant. Which one are you dealing with?

Maneesha: Humble and friendly by default, Maneesha has a warm smile.

♀ FEMALE

Mango: A full-blown hippy-chick.

Manon: The name of an apron as worn by a Belgian peasant woman in a village kitchen that is gripped by a freezing northern European winter, 300 years ago.

Marayke: Here is another case of a name being so 'out there' that this is exactly where her destiny took her. Marayke is a sensuous mystery, but the last time anyone heard of her, she was studying gorillas in Uganda. Has anyone heard from her since?

Marcia: Whinges heaps.

Marcy: A gifted mathematician and physicist. There are planets out there beyond Pluto that need discovering, not to mention the sun's incredible ejections of plasma whose effect on the Earth needs further investigation. Indeed, we're lucky to have her.

Maree: Garlic, and if you don't love the stuff please leave the kitchen immediately.

Marg: Marg also goes by the names of Mrs. Reliable and Mrs. Thank Christ That's Over With.

Margaret: An Australian sheep dog. A Border Collie. A legend. Loved by all and feared by sheep. What we do without her? *What would Australia do without her?*

Margarita: The name of a huge multi-coloured beach-ball that is tossed about by thirty male and female models, who happen to be gleefully running down a sand dune in the name of making a TV ad for Coca-Cola.

Margot: Margot is as sexy as hell but there are no beg pardons here: Got a problem? Go to Margo. Her honesty may be too much for some but the world needs her.

Marguerite: Beautiful and mixed up.

Margie: If you're in a room and she's in the one, next door, if she laughs you'll know because you won't be able to concentrate on what you are doing, or watching. On a quiet night you'll even hear her if she's inside at the front of the house and you're out in the backyard.

Margy: See Margie.

Maria: Her mum taught her to cook and that's great, but that isn't one five hundredth of the story. And she loves with all her might.

Marianna: "Oh, daaarling. It's sooooo good to seeeeeee you....!!!! Here.....crack this. Oooohhh, you look simply divine!!" .....etc, etc.

Marianne: See Maryanne.

Marie: After you harm yourself in some way (ie. via an Angela, a Brittany or a Kay) there is roughly one second during which you wait for the pain to actually arrive. This is called the Marie Period. They're not much fun (although they are adrenalin filled, and therefore exciting in some sadistic way) but they're a fact of life.

Marieka: A picture of pointed neatness and eccentric grace.

Marika: With the subtle eccentricities of a Northern European background, Marika is more committed and conservative than you might expect.

Marilyn: Marilyn is another woman who can't help escape a certain kind of maleness, but she is a sensual woman and one whose tough and dignified skin hides a girly sense of fun.

♀ FEMALE

Marina: Marina's line of argument is occasionally out of whack with the truth, which is a shame because she's a passionate soul on the continual march for righteousness.

Marion: Marion is a deeply sensual and funny woman. At a quick glance you might think that she'd be morose and slightly timid, but that couldn't be further from the truth. She'll take your breath away.

Marita: Marita is an energetic woman who harnesses that energy in being able to fix or clean-up almost any situation that requires it, and it assists her in being a wonderful friend that dishes out prudent advice when needed. (She dances on tables when she's drunk.)

Marissa: Highly active and therefore generally lean of limb and lovely, Marissa could be the radio DJ with a high-pitched voice who laughs at nothing and laughs at nothing (which isn't perfect), as easily as she might be the sharp-talking business owner who can't handle watching a second wasted. Either way, Marissa relishes being the Queen of the Stage.

Marj: A more relaxed and potent version of her daughter, below.

Marjorie: A splendid country mother who wins the Shepherd's Pie baking competition at the show, each year. It's just too delicious.

Marlee: Like a scenario out of a movie, if a nuclear warhead detonated above Sydney then all that would humanly remain would be a scared and filthy little girl with bright tough eyes, and whose name was Marlee.

Marlene: The beautiful pragmatist with a wonderful sense of humour. Marlene is possibly the unsung backbone of rural Australian life.

Marlin: No, she may not be from around these parts but Marlin is a woman who knows how to use her powers.

Marnie: You look down into the deep dark well and you yell, "Helloooooooooooo.........." You listen, waiting for the echo to return to you and tell you how deep it is. How deep is it? How deep is the well?

Martine: Is she a mild misfit or just a magnet for eerie coincidences? She might even be positively schizophrenic but beneath the confusion there lies a kind heart and a deeply sexual undertone.

Mary: The thick woollen jumper that you put on when it's freezing cold. She's comforting and intelligent, sensual and unusual, she smells incredible, she's everyone's favourite and she's the dark horse of the century – no question. However, Mary does carry a hidden burden....

Maryanne: Soft at the beginning and hard at the finish, Maryanne is the sort of girl that will start a fight just so she can join in. She swears like a cow cocky.

Mary-Lou: Do we expect a mystery or not? Is she wise? Is she a dim-witted buffoon? No one is sure, but there is a high probability that she works in a lolly shop.

Matilda: Matilda is too bloody nice and wonderful for her own good.

Maureen: See the male George.

♀ FEMALE

Max: Max is a reasonably normal superstar whose only possible gripe is the maleness that the world attributes to her. Not that she *has* a gripe, to be honest, because she carries one of the most independent and powerful names in the Kingdom that provides her with intelligence and spunk. (Gentlemen, if you believe in marriage then you could do a lot worse.)

Maxy: The cheeky, horny, drunk or aggressive version of Max, above.

Maxine: A-type personality, or maybe an A-B. Maxine is highly intelligent, a natural leader and she is enthused by unusual people and preposterous situations.

May: May would have had a lot more fun if she'd been in her 20's during the 60's, rather than in her 30's during the 40's, as was the case, but I suppose there was no food back then. In any case, May is honest, respectable and direct.

Maya: Maya was re-incarnated from a Central American Goddess that lived 1500 years ago in what is known today as Costa Rica. She has perfect olive skin, luscious black hair, a devilish smile in her dark eyes and she holds a PhD in quantum chemistry, which has everything to do with how she was re-incarnated in the first place.

Mayiwase: (Pron. Maa-why-say) Like many many people, she ain't originally from around these parts, which is a grand thing (apart from all Kiwis). Anyway, Mayiwase laughs loudly, studies hard and provides a different tweak on how to do things.

Maytal: Maytal rhymes with Just Right.
She has a diamond stud through her nose, potent Israeli blood in her veins and delicious green bliss in her eyes.

Meaghan: Completely underrated, Meaghan has a warm heart and she is true to the bone. Like Blue Tongue lizards and Wedge Tailed Eagles, she borders on being another Australian icon.

Meg: Like any new wooden clothes peg, Meg is elemental, unpolished and she has chores to attend to.

Megan: (Pron. Meg-ann) Megan carries a blunt tomahawk and enjoys chopping wood for long periods.

Mel: She's more of a man than Troy, Spencer and Perry put together, but somehow she manages to retain her woman's sexiness. She'll often vent any personal frustration by insisting that any friends that happen to be present wrestle her in a no-holds-barred affair. Win or lose, you will be covered in bruises at the finish and you'll be lucky if you can use your wrist the next day, but she'll be the first person to buy you a beer at the pub afterwards.

Melanie: 'Melanie' is what you say when you accidentally inhale seawater while swimming in the ocean, but there's a lesson in everything, apparently. Melanie, herself, aspires to grow organic vegetables and avoid confrontations.

Melina: Melina never accepts your answer as the answer.

Melinda: Tomato sauce. Most boys love her and even those people who aren't a fan will tolerate her presence, no worries.

Melisa: Melisa isn't unlike her older and more responsible sister, below, except that she's more unpredictable. For example, she loves taking pictures of her naked tattooed boyfriend while he's asleep, which is something Melissa would only do if she was hyper-excited and/or tipsy.

♀ FEMALE

Melissa: Melissa is normal gal with a warm, loving nature and she hardly ever suffers from psychotic episodes.

Melita: Melita reads the rules before she acts and the recipe before she cooks. With a little luck, she will come back in another life as Nancy, and learn how not to do things.

Melody: A rather sexy Juggernaut.

Mem: Her name resembles an individual hiccup, so something in her life is going to be seriously out of whack, sometime, but Mem's spirited sense of *joi de vivre* will always see her right because greatness nearly always results from adversity.

Meng: Jazz singer, beat boxer and naked gardener – you name it – Meng is a gorgeous brute of a woman.

Mercedes: Life's tougher challenges.....is she up to it? Initially, one thinks not but then, the girl turns into a woman, and all of a sudden the swan emerges from the gloom and the graceful lines of her thinking propel her forward. Mercedes is a serious and regal cat, sure enough, but she's down-pat with the things that matter...

Meredith: A beautiful woman. She used to be a manic-depressive who couldn't believe people in the world were so cruel. Nowadays, she pines to be a mother because she thinks motherhood will solve all her problems. She's wrong, it won't, but at least it's a course of action.

Meri: A cross between a mild case of Bali Belly (whose worst symptom is that it gives you something to think about) and a bed covered in the petals of red Spanish roses, Meri propels herself into the universe rather splendidly because she expects that great things will happen.

Merva: Merva the Perva.

Mery: Mary's unforgiving, complicated and loving cousin whose origins hail from the passionate Adriatic.

Mhairi: A Gaelic nightmare.

Mia: Mia is a mound of fairy floss that you buy on a stick at the show. She is therefore very sweet and too much of her might make you ill.

Micah: Precise in her movements; Punctual; Thoughtful. Micah has the most looked-after skin in the Kingdom which has the effect of making her resemble someone half her age. Little do most people know, however, that Micah can carry the world on her shoulders.

Michaela: Michaela is the name of any haircut that goes 'Voomph' across the forehead and 'Voom-Voomph' down the sides.

Michelle: Michelle is the name given to the sound of little waves washing up on a tiny coral atoll. And that's great, so long as you arrived there on a dive trip or some other planned adventure, and not via a shipwreck or plane crash.

Michka: The name of a type of dream where everything starts off great and then ends in utter catastrophe, possibly your own death.

Miho: True to form, Miho is the Japanese term for an incredibly long and wonderful sailing journey. What a girl she is...

Mika: Sexy, contained and diligent with a gentle swish of self consciousness washed over it all, Mika is lovely.

♀ FEMALE

Mikala: Mikala is obsessive-compulsive in at least one aspect of her life – possibly with regard to cleaning.

Milli: If Milli isn't a cutesy-wootsie little puppy dog, then she is a gorgeous blonde human from the Czech Republic. In the case of the latter, whatever you do, don't ask her if she's from Czechoslovakia because that doesn't exist anymore. I'm just warning you... (The Australian versions are much less dangerous.)

Mimi: Mimi is the terrified squeak as muttered by a fluffy white rabbit that is fleeing the huntsman's shotgun.

Min: A short name for an intricate personality, and one that folds over, in on itself, like a new born baby cuddled-up in its cot in slumber. On the surface Min is gregarious, generous, worldly and incisive but all the while, deep down, she aches to be happy, and to be loved. It seems that most people in the Kingdom wish for the same thing.

Miranda: Neat, prissy and fussy. Miranda is nice until she's angry although that can be said of most of us. She detests fishy smells and wearing the same clothes two days in a row.

Mirella: Mirella lets all the crap that doesn't matter sail past her without so much as a second thought. She's cool, she's funny, she gets it, and she's great at assisting others to see the moral of the story.

Miriam: Passionate for love and life, Miriam is an incredible optimist. Nothing gets her down. Nothing. In short, Miriam is a bloody legend.

Miss Mango: The name of Ruth's vagina.

Missy: Provocative.

Mo: Right, well, you better strap yourself into the seat of your roller coaster properly because there is an 11% chance of it coming off the rails, so try to enjoy the ride. (Note: Mo has a not-so-secret penchant for Big Trucks. She thinks they are, "Orgasmic!")

Moira: The naughty little girl with freckles, who steals the odd toffee apple from the local milk bar.

Molly: Molly is that deliciously satisfying feeling you get after you rouse from bed in the morning, having made love all night long, and having had plenty of good sleep afterwards.

Mon: Whatever she's doing - and she generally does everything easily and with a simple grace - she needs to be married before she has kids. It's just how she is.

Monica: The inner tube of a tractor tyre that the kids inflate and take down to the lake to play with. And that's all wonderful, but occasionally they return home with nasty scrapes from the valve that sticks out rather rudely.

Monique: The living embodiment of a chook raffle.

Mora: See Morah.

Morag: Light-hearted and compassionate, Morag is in the Top 10 most dependable people in the Kingdom.

Morah: Irish or not, behind the dusty curtain is a no-nonsense thunderbolt of sexiness, calm and humour.

♀ FEMALE

Morgan: Morgan believes she belongs on the edge of a polo field in her designer clothes, somewhere, doing whatever it is they do there. Is that the English form of cheerleading?

Mummacat: Mummacat is young at heart and she doesn't take herself too seriously. As you might expect, however, she'd walk over hot coals and lift trucks for her children who are encouraged and loved to greatness and beyond.

Mumsie: The relaxed know-it-all.

Muriel: No one knows this so keep it to yourself.....in fact, come close so I can whisper it to you......*did you know that Muriel is actually a superhero?.....and her real name is....Muriel the Underdog.*

Myla: Part Malaysian, part Indian and probably part English, Myla has gorgeous long black hair that she tosses over the back of any comfy chair that she happens to be reclining in. In this position she will listen attentively to anyone who is speaking unless she thinks they are full of shit, in which case, she will sink further down into her seat and contemplate what kinds of fabric she might buy during her upcoming trip to Indonesia.

Mylie: Mylie tries to be smiley but she stresses herself out all the time by attempting to make her mind up about things as quickly as possible.

Myrrhine: Some way between Miriam and Marilyn, Myrrhine is exotic and incisive, and not to be taken lightly. She's the kind of girl who, if accidentally walking into the wrong theatre to watch a play that was never happening, and where a string quartet was playing instead, would take it upon herself to shmooze her way into one of the boxes where there was champagne, binoculars and an after-performance party.

Nadia: Nadia walks carefully, even on flat ground, but here's a question: What comes first, the chicken or the egg? How is a young girl supposed to behave (and therefore evolve) under the weight and expectation of a name intended for a highly educated and demure 40 year old? (Unless, of course, she is the happiest person in the Kingdom, in which case everything turned out to be perfect.)

Nadine: Her name is so ridiculous that she is exactly not what one might anticipate. Cooler than she sounds and definitely sexier, Nadine is unusually delicious.

Naila: Naila makes up the numbers in a completely inoffensive (if not unmemorable) manner.

Nancy: Her name is as pure as the driven snow and behind this alibi she gets away with a huge variety of wonderful sins. Nancy, God bless you.

Nanette: Demanding. Busy.

Naomi: Picture this: You're walking home while carrying one of those cool-looking carry bags from an expensive fashion store. You didn't buy that much and so the bag isn't that full but because it's a windy day it's almost impossible to walk without the bag blowing all over the place, at times nearly carrying you off balance or getting caught behind your legs. This phenomenon is called the Naomi Effect, and she has a pointy nose.

Narelle: A wild boar that lives in the forest. She has big tusks, she grunts and, generally, she is a contented soul in her strange little world. Like Jodie, she's only really dangerous when cornered.

♀ FEMALE

Nat: Nat is as cool as shit, and she cruises through life with the ease and grace of the bow of a cruise ship slicing the blue, warm tropical waters of the Coral Sea. Nice work Nat.

Natalia: Natalia is a nice wholesome girl, but she freaks out if she spies so much as the hint of a hair in her armpits, an out-of-place hair on her eyebrows or crutch, and if she spotted a dark hair on her upper-lip there is a fair chance she would consider suicide.

Natalie: The Swiss Army knife that's ready to stab, cut, unscrew, slice, grip, open, scale, magnify and abrade anything that needs it. Unfortunately, she has so many functions that she sometimes forgets what to use when. The last time I saw her she was trying to cut through a wire fence with a screwdriver. Strangely, she's probably the only one who can crack the *Craig Conundrum*.

Natasha: A gifted ice-speed skater who is fit, competitive and full of guile. She'll share a joke with you before and after a race but just take notice; if you fall during the contest and forget to pull your fingers into a fist as you hit the ice, if you are in her way you can expect to lose at least a couple of them. (She does love the sight of other peoples' blood.)

Nathalie: Nathalie is essentially identical to Natalie, except that she is slightly better at dealing with unexpected chaos.

Neisha: The elegant and sexy Ibis bird who hits her target every time, and with the greatest of ease.

Nelly: Nelly arrived here with the First Fleet and she's just about fed-up of having to wear a triple-layered dress, long sleeves and a bonnet in the middle of the Australian summer. Irrespective of that disaster, she can drive a team of bullocks, build fences, deliver babies and she can manually milk even a disgruntled cow in her sleep.

Nerida: Regardless – or perhaps, because – she carries a supremely divine personal aura, Nerida is trained in the classical arts and the classical airs.

Nic: Nic is an empowered woman who, apart from her generally gorgeous look, is full of true grit. Once she makes her mind up about something, there's no turning back.

Niccole: Like many before and after her, she detests her name being misspelt and, despite being an ostensibly good and intelligent person, this spills over into her life in the form of a peculiar kind of impatience.

Nickers: To carry such as a blasé name can only mean that Nickers has a huge IQ and a determination to get things done. And so it is. Did I mention that she's also a bit saucy?

Nicky: Nicky is similar to her more dashing cousin with the short nickname, except that she's a little more humble, and a little more rural.

Nicola: Intense and solemn like an encyclopaedia in a library, Nicola means well but she has twisted ideas about men and about the world. With lots of unconditional love, however, she'll be fine.

Nicole: The Nicole is the name of a quiet prayer uttered by nuns all over the world every Friday night. They pray that they have the strength to resist the desire to go out and socialise, and to meet boys.

Nien: Nien is so inoffensive that she puts people to sleep.

Nik: See Nic, although this one has a much higher probability of having blonde hair.

♀ FEMALE

Nikki: 90% of Nikki's are blonde – it's a fact of nature – and men adore them because they are attracted to all bright and shiny objects, and blonde hair reflects more light than most, but don't be fooled by the cute name. Beneath Nikki's sweet and sensual exterior is a core that is incredibly tough and flexible. (Oddly enough, occasionally it's the reverse and we love her for it, either way.)

Nina: With a star sign of a Leo or a Taurus, maybe Scorpio, Nina is a French secret agent. She's an expert in hand to hand combat, speaks eleven languages, can dismantle a AK-47 in about three seconds flat and she currently holds the record for *le bisou du matin* – The Morning Kiss. (A race that involves climbing the steps of the Eiffel Tower to the main viewing platform and base-jumping from it.) And she stops any room that she walks into.

Niya: Niya is a wonderful breath of fresh air who provides a calming and friendly influence.

Noelene: A stock standard Australian kangaroo. Red or Grey, it doesn't matter, and she wears an ambivalent smile on her face whether things have gone to shit or not. "Fuck, that's inappropriate," she'll say, if they have.

Noni: The name given to the final product in a secretive game of pass the parcel. The question is, *who is she?* And, *will she be worth the wait?*

Nonie: Nonie likes playing a game that is some combination of the one involving her sister, above, with that of her other sister, below. In order to do that one assumes that she is interesting, cluey, sexy and a mixture of all the good things. (And just as her sisters are, as a matter of fact).

Nonny: Nonny is a funny and irreverent soul who loves playing sexual dress-up games. She's great company and good in a crisis.

Nora: Like manure for the garden, Nora is enriching in all but the most obvious of ways.

Norafiah: The outgoing fitness freak and body builder who stands out in a crowd. Gemini.

Noreen: Picture this: It's just gone sunrise, mist fills the bottom of the valley and all is peaceful on the farm. Way back at the far end of the property there is a lone bull standing in a paddock. He has a stainless steel ring through his nose and he is a magnificent creature. In the still of the morning haze, he lifts up his great head, takes a long breath of air and then bellows out into the morning chill, "Nooooorreeeeeeeeeeeeeeeeeeeeeen......??"

Nori-Jae: Highly competitive with a big ego, Nori-Jae will use all and any means available in order to get her way.

Nyanda: Nyanda is lovely but she's too polite to every-body.

Nyree: The Nyree is the name of a pub about 300km north west of Birdsville. Trackers, truckers, roustabouts and outback desert folk go there for beer and steak n' chips.

Oleta: Trouble.

Olga: Olga is big and tough, and as an Olympic discus thrower from St Petersburg, Russia, she needs to be.

♀ **FEMALE**

Olive: "Olive, I have a problem," you say, and she sits quietly and listens while you tell her your woes. After you have finished she leans forward and takes your hands in hers, and explains how it is, how the world works, and what you can do to make your problem go away. Thankyou Olive.

Olivia: An Olivia Incident is the rather tragic phenomenon of two sports cars crashing, head-on. Before that, though, life is ideal. Perfect, even.

Olwyn: Olwyn rhymes with, "What, another one? Oh well.... alright then." As a phrase muttered regularly by midwives, secretaries and personal assistants all over the planet, daily, without her the modern world would surely struggle.

Ophelia: Ophelia is a curvaceous woman who seduces young men by telling them that she never wears any knickers.

Oprah: The name of a huge dining table made out of solid American Oak. She was built where she sits and it takes 10 men to move her now, but by god has she seen some sights? She's had food and all manner of grog tossed all over her, presidents, queens and the odd homeless person have feasted in her presence, and raunchy guests have fornicated on and under her.

Paige: Paige is the name given to a cup of Earl Grey tea that's been left too long. It would have been lovely had it been drunk sooner but now it's cold, and is there anything more offensively drab than a cold cup of tea?

Pam: Pam rhymes with Puffed Up.
Botox, silicon breasts, liposuction – you name it, she's done it. Her and her bleached blonde hair live in Noosa with a drug lord and she's actually pretty chilled out about it, but not about everything else.

Pamela: Pamela picked up a very nice Mercedes Benz from her divorce and she kept the house. She re-married her lawyer.

Paris: The name of a fancy pair of red knickers.

Pat: The General.

Patrice: Cute, sexy, and blah blah blah. However, you will do well to go out of your way in order to stay on her good side as she is otherwise intolerable. Is she dangerous in this situation?? I don't know.....probably.

Patricia: Patricia exercises madly but she hit her straps in the fee love days of the 60's. The Beatles, beards, weed – it was all there – and she's a laid back character now because of it. (Despite all the exercise.)

Patti: The deceptively potent Leader of the Pack.

Paula: Paula is beautiful and she is charismatic, and she only just scraped passed the disaster without getting caught up in it. So, take a breath and relax baby.......you made it!

Pauline: Antiseptic solution. Keep in the cupboard.

Peachy: Peachy lives for getting tipsy and going skinny-dipping in the middle of the night.

Pearl: Built to cope with adversity, Pearl is harder on the outside than she is in the middle.

Peggy: What a life-giving babbling ball of bloody fun and love and splendid carry-on, she is.

Petrina: Petrina walks the walk, she talks the talk, she's sufficiently sensually picture-perfect and she takes no shit. You go girl!

♀ FEMALE

Penelope: A full-bodied woman who has one of the most powerful voices in the Kingdom. She showers outside in her luscious garden whilst singing to her heart's content and the townsfolk can hear her from miles away, although they think the same of her as anyone who meets her for the first time: that Penelope is highly talented, incredibly sexy and supremely wonderful.

Penn: More sensitive than she sounds or seems, Penn is supremely reliable in all manner of situations. Improbably sexy, also. Her high level of intelligence is virtually a given.

Penni: See Penny.

Penny: Penny is energetic and she means well, never flinching at a poor reaction to one or more of her directions, because *who else* is going to tell the fools how to behave and/or clean up after themselves?

Peta: All of us have issues of some variety and Peta's stem from having to repeatedly prove her femininity to the world. Not that she gives a shit, really, but the result is a tough and independent hombre.

Pettina: The Prissy Gameplayer.

Petula: A staunch catholic.

Phillipa: Phillipa has the annoying habit of answering other peoples' questions for them, especially when she's bored. As a child she insisted that all of her friends play her games exactly as she intended and, in adulthood, nothing much has changed.

Phyllis: Phyllis is as rough as guts but she hugs harder than anyone.

Phoebe: Her father is certifiably insane, which explains why Phoebe is as complicated as she is. So it's not her fault, classically speaking, but Phoebe is pretty cool. Keep an eye on her if you like, but she'll be fine.

Pia: Maximally attentive and lovely, Pia exists here in this moment, all the time. It's an impressive skill.

Pip: Perfect to take into battle, Pip is passionate and single-minded, her decisions are made in a flash and her general level of sexiness makes the outcomes of such decisions even better….generally.

Pippa: Borderline adrenaline junkie. As one of the few female bullfighters in existence, she loves being in the centre of the arena where her decisions really matter, and where she can singlehandedly thrill the crowd.

Po: Po is centred, spiritually content and intelligently poised, and all of this makes her even more attractive than she already is. Indeed, Po deserves a round of applause….

Polly: You wake up really late and leap out of bed before running out the door while still half asleep: this is called the Polly Moment. It feels crazy, painful and illogical at the start but everything turns out to be wonderful in the end. It always does.

Poppy: Poppy is hard to miss and impossible to ignore. She has excellent posture and she always gets what she wants.

Precious: Prima donna.

Priscilla: Naive but completely honourable.

♀ FEMALE

Princess: Princess is one of the most potent female names and not just anyone can pull it off. Indeed, it's not possible for an individual to carry the name Princess, and not *actually be* some kind of Princess. In short, Princess is physically and spiritually beautiful and, without doubt, she is one of the funniest human beings you'll ever meet.

Prue: Prue was born on a planet that exists light years from earth and she arrived here in a space ship, which is why she might seem a little odd. Nowadays, having never acclimatised to our stronger gravitational field, she is always very thin and she struggles with any kind of physical exertion. This actually provides her with great comfort for so long as she is thought of as being anorexic and frail she will always be thought of as being human, and this is all she ever wanted. (She's not the least bit dangerous.)

Quentin: She shares her male counterpart's intelligence and unusualness, except that she is so ideally happy within herself and her world that she almost belies belief. Quentin is amazing. She would have made an excellent grief counsellor.

Quinn: Quinn is softer than her male counterpart but is she a sensitive loner? Do still waters run deep, or do they just sit there? Maybe the water is actually quite shallow but the angle of the sun makes it look mysteriously dark and irresistibly inviting?

Rachael: Option A: The Queen of Eroticism.

Option B: Sir Isaac Newton said that every action has an equal and opposite reaction, and for everyone else this is probably true. Her name is soft and tender, and perhaps it permits other to feel like they can treat her harshly and get away with it? I'm not sure. Perhaps this is why she suffers more bad luck than most?

Rachel: See Rachael.

Rae: Boxer. She turned pro three years ago, wins every bout inside two rounds and carries a mean right hook. As a tough man in a recent past life, she's desperately sad that she can't urinate without consequence while standing up, in this one.

Raelene: Raelene sticks her head out the back door with a cigarette in one hand, a rum and coke in the other, and screams at her five dishevelled-looking children in the back yard, "GET OFF THE CLOTHES LINE.... AND UNTIE THE BLOODY CAT!"

Ramona: Dramatic. If she ever cries about anything you can hear her wailing from down the street.

Rania: Like a double-sided mirror that is perfectly clean and with extremely sharp edges, Rania is two-faced and vindictive in her ignorance.

Rebecca: Rebecca is a gifted intellectual who should be making the most of her excellent upbringing. Far sexier than anyone might gauge from just looking at her, and like Mary before her, Rebecca can be a wonderful dark horse. However, there is a chance that she is actually a race horse wearing blinkers, in which case she can be incredibly frustrating, if not completely deluded. See how you go...

Rechelle: The world deems Rechelle to be a naturally glittering superstar Goddess of a persona, who simply doesn't feel like have anything to do with the music industry, and whose smile and nature gravitate people and energy toward her. Rechelle, on the other hand, thinks she's just Rechelle. (Both parties are correct.)

Red: Wow!...... Just.. wow!!

♀ FEMALE

Regi: Regi is open and loving, and ready to rock n' roll at a moment's notice.

Remedius: The Healer.

Remi: Gifted. Effervescent. Loving

Renie: The graceful artist. You can find her curled over her work in quiet concentration, forgetting the world while she strives, but all of us wait for her to leap up and burst into bloom. What a day that will be.

Renee: The Pakistani bus that's full of people and careering down a mountain road, having lost the function of its brakes. The 70 people crammed on board are screaming in horror because they know that they're about to die a bloody and violent death. And they're right. They do.

Reshma: Like the soothing sounds of a babbling brook, Reshma is the wise and peaceful rock for those that are lucky enough to know her. No, you won't see her throwing her knickers at a rock star performing on stage in front of her, but you could easily see her receiving a bravery award for saving the life of a drowning man she happened to spot while she was walking her dog along the beach.

Resi: Resi burns incredibly brightly but not forever. She's a knockout in a scarlet dress.

Rhani: Rhani is gentle, sensual, agile and noble. She might even be a little bit too gentle.....

Rhian: See Robert

FEMALE ♀

Rhiannon: She's quiet and she's not, and her seductive eyelashes hide a more acute acumen than is visible to the eye. Secret schemes are afoot here and she camouflages her controlling nature very well.

Rho: Her parents could have named her Theta, Gamma or Psi, and the result would have been similar. Rho is an unusual, specially educated and eclectic woman who deals with things like publishing houses and production companies, and who enjoys the finer things in life.

Rhona: A normal lady who has led an interesting life and raised a proud family. She lives for scrabble.

Rhonda: The hopeless romantic. If you believe in reincarnations, then understand that Rhonda had been around many times before, although she's still desperately searching. She seems very close to achieving what she's always wanted but will this life prove to be the one? She does have lots of beautiful thick hair though – that's nearly always a given.

Rie: Rie is one of those rare individuals in the Kingdom who exudes a strange and electric aura that calms, soothes and rejuvenates. That makes her something of a Goddess.

Rihanna: Cabbage soup (I know! Why don't we all just move to Alabama, go on the doll, eat nothing but quarter pounders and start shootin' stuff?).

Rikki: Rikki is in your face.

Rimma: Optimistic. Unpredictable.

♀ FEMALE

Rina: With a name similar to a famous Sicilian gangster, Rina is a well-oiled, beautifully maintained, seductively intriguing and absolutely lethal cross-bow.

Rita: As an attractive woman with very angular features, Rita lives a streamlined life. She recognizes yet-to-be-friends in an instant and lavishes them with love and attention, while she is polite to those she deems a fool. Rest assured, however, that people in the latter category mysteriously find themselves never encountering her again. It's one of her great skills.

Ro: Ro doesn't have time or the inclination to buy things like sexy skirts, expensive perfume or matching underwear because she's too busy getting-on and dealing with the things that matter – ie. friends, jeans, beer etc.

Robbie: Robbie gives her all.

Roberta: Roberta rhymes with Out There.
Commercial pilot, cigar smoker, deep-sea diver and tattooist for a while; she's done it all. But (mothers, fathers, boyfriends and others) don't expect her to marry.

Robin: Robin lives on a farm in Poland that grows potatoes when the soil isn't frozen. She has short hair.

Robyn: See Robin, except Robyn dresses more conserv-atively.

Rochelle: Oh Rochelle......she's lovely but what's all this fussing about??

Ronelle: Gorgeous and seductive, Ronelle is *so* cool that she's got the letter 'R' tattooed above her right breast.

Ronnie: Tall, slim and slender, Ronnie is as beautiful as she is temperamental. She might even be *incredibly* temperamental, if not highly prejudicial.

Rosa: Rosa is short in stature, of Italian descent and she has beautiful eyes. However, DO NOT anger her unless you feel like being on the receiving end of a beating. (Hello Rosa, you look wonderful, by the way! xx)

Rosalie: Her name starts off okay then it immediately crashes awkwardly – in the same way that you might turn and walk away from a friend that you happened upon while you were down the street, trip over the edge of the curb that you forgot was there, fall onto the road and be hit by a cyclist who is travelling fast enough for them to break your arm. (At least it's not a car, or something bigger.)

Rosanna: High maintenance, no limits and great fun to hang out with 69% of the time. You can always sleep later.

Ros: In the movie, Pulp Fiction, Harvey Keitel plays a character called the Wolf, who comes in to clean up a catastrophic mess with a determined ease, and with style. Had they made the movie in Australia and called the (female) character Ros or Roz, instead, nothing would have changed.

Rose: Spiritual, sensual and highly intelligent, Rose has a big personality. She is the kind of girl who rides a very old pushbike, and who has no compunction in kicking men out of her bed as soon as she has finished with them.

♀ FEMALE

Rosemary: Whenever Rosemary walks into the room, if you listen closely, you can hear the angels trumpet her arrival from above. (In reality, however, and unless you have the hearing of a beagle, you will only be aware of the sound as a subliminal and inner sense of peace, happiness and relief.)

Rosie: What a chick. Rosie is a modern, extravagant, fun-loving legend who will beat the living shit out of anyone that pisses her off.

Rosita: "Rozzzzzzitaaaaaa.....!!!!!!!" her friends will squeal as she walks into the room because, finally, the glorious whirly-bird has arrived!

Rowena: Rowena is just as happy in a bar of bush blokes as she is in front of the camera signing billion dollar deals with offshore mining companies. If you are genuine then she will give you your due and if you're not, she will either ignore you or tell you to fuck off. Rowena.

Roxy: A type of Impulse spray for girls. It's a fav-ourite with some sixteen year olds who cover themselves in it before heading out to nightclubs, underage, although it only really works when the accompanying mini-skirts are so short that any attempt to sit down results in a genuine knicker-flash.

Roz: See Ros.

Ruby: Ruby lives alone with her 45 cats in a house filled with ornaments and trinkets from her two trips to India. She hopes to achieve enlightenment soon but little does she know that she's on life number one.

Ruth: The champion shearer. She beats all the men all the time, and she wouldn't trade her love of ciggies, Wild Turkey or her blue Chesty Bond singlets to save her life.

Ruwani: The lazy and beautiful Sri Lankan Goddess of Safe Animals.

Sabina: Canadian. Which means she doesn't like too much bad language, although she is always looking for more sex than she's getting. Who doesn't?

Sabine: Made of silver and about 21cm long, Sabine is gorgeous to look at and wonderful to hold. When Elizabeth is hosting a formal dinner party, she polishes her like no-tomorrow because Sabine is a main course dinner fork, and is there no better fork in the world? I think not.

Sabrina: As a very successful executioner, she wears the same sexy smile for both her best friends and her worst enemies.

Sacha: The name of a super-plush velvet rug that is deep purple in colour, and desired to be rolled upon, naked, by any and all who her meet her.

Sal: Picture a female version of Bruce Willis in any of the Die Hard movies. Especially the first one.

Sally: Energetic and complex, Sally pursues unusual projects and unusual men, which is the product of quite an acute acumen. She can often be seen sipping at her 5th coffee of the morning while staring out into space where she's analyses all manner of philosophy. We think.

♀ FEMALE

Sally-Anne: If a biscuit is dunked in tea or coffee for too long it will come apart in the liquid, and a large portion of the biscuit will be sacrificed to the God of Hot Drinks. The immersion time needed to achieve catastrophic absorption of the liquid into the biscuit and thereby reach a point of no return in terms of a safe extraction is known as the Sally-Anne Time. It's otherwise known as the S.A.T and it's something that can only be avoided by trial and error.

Sam: It has been almost impossible for Sam to shake the Tom Boy image but it's made her an outdoorsy sort of person who is smart on her feet. She's quite gifted at orienteering and it helps that she has an excellent sense of smell, although she doesn't take to the dainty types too well – be they men or women.

Samantha: A neat woman who fusses more than she needs to. No one knows what Samantha does for a living but she takes a lot of pride in having good hair and getting absolutely hammered on Friday night.

Samara: Like a tribal bonfire in a remote PNG mountain village, we expect her to be exotic and mysterious but the most we can say is that she is attentive and reasonably conservative.

Sami: Sami struggles with shy people, she snorts when she laughs and she sneezes and farts loudly.

Sandra: Purposeful, attractive and occasionally aloof, she'll do her thing and she'll do it extremely well.

Sandy: Relaxed and affable, earthy and sexy as well, Sandy's fate is that she will give birth to a child-genius that will subsequently make her life far more complex than she ever planned. But, it'll take a relaxed and interesting person to deal with it. (Don't let her maleness bother you, gentlemen, for Sandy is lovely.)

FEMALE ♀

Sangeeta: Serene and gorgeous, Sangeeta is one of the most elegant and thoughtful creatures in the Kingdom.

Sara: There is a train of thought in the scientific and archaeological world that Sara is actually the reincarnation of Cleopatra. (Certainly, 49% of Saras assume this to be the case.)

Sarah: A prototype model of perfection. She tries not to offend people but sometimes it can't be helped. Thoughtful, philosophical, generous and very sexy on her day, Sarah is generally an impatient cook.

Sarah-Jane: SJ has no idea what normal people do and, while you'd never pick it, beneath the suave exterior is a gifted audiovisual artist who is quite insane. She once planned to spend six months in a tank full or water before she made the decision to pursue a career as an astronaut. And she'll do it too. You watch.

Sari-Anne: An Indonesian drink. For all the dry bitterness in her name – and her capacity to hold a grudge – she can party till dawn.

Sarina: The name of a marquee above a well-partied wedding reception. She provides plenty of space and light and she is quite accustomed to being in the company of melodramatic drunkards at midnight. Strong wind and rain make her ill at ease, though, and in such a mood it is best if no one says anything to provoke any kind of reaction.

Sarz: Sexy Sarz is one of the more highly vibrational people in the Kingdom.

Sasha: In scientific terms you might call Sasha spoilt but like her kindred spirit, Declan, the universe simply affords her plenty without her needing to do very much, and that's okay. Surely someone in the Kingdom has to be?

♀ FEMALE

Scarlett: A vixen from head to tail. Forget common sense - who needs it? Passionate in both love and hate, she delights in wearing bright colours, especially in her predominantly red hair.

Sekai: Like her kindred spirit, above, Sekai almost certainly has flaming red hair, but she's flat-out as wild as fuck. A magnificent effort, Madame Sekai.

Serena: Serena travels a lot for work and she knows all the rorts. She has wardrobe full of towels and soaps from hotels from all over the world, and only a fair recollection of the men that she left pining in her wake after her. "Oh well," she'll say, after just recovering from the last conference. "Where are we off to next?"

Shae: Often very fit and healthy, Shae is a nice lady in some kind of a hurry.

Shaina: Nope, she doesn't look 'normal' and nor should she. Shaina gives no quarter, she takes no prisoner and whether it's because of her looks or her nature, she always leaves behind her a wake worth remembering.

Shandra: The Shandra is an ancient spell that women used to employ to have the men of their desires fall hopelessly in love with them. Sadly, it died out during the middle ages when the Europeans decided to burn all their witches. Or did they?

Shannon: Like Courtney, Shannon has a lot more grunt than her male counterpart. So much so, in fact, that she's often thought of as being damn-near pig-headed and this is unfair. She's just complex and driven, and there's nothing wrong with that.

Sharelle: A well-adjusted, shit-giving Aussie girl who has a stack of friends, noble ambitions and a firm grasp on reality.

Sharlene: Sharlene murdered her boyfriend in a fit of P.M.T. and she's currently on the run in either South America or Cabramatta. If only she'd become show jumper like she wanted to do when she was a little girl, things might have been okay.

Sharman: Sharman is a surprising name but there are no surprises here. Whatever her appearance, underneath Sharman's skin is a gruff male witchdoctor from the island nation of Haiti.

Sharna: Very close to the coveted land of exotica, Sharna actually rhymes with 'Shit, that's sharp!' and 'Oh, bugger it, I think I've lost my sunnies...'

Sharon: A traditional bowl of porridge.

Sharyn: Sharyn has no time to waste, and she loathes it when people spell her name with an 'o'.

Shaugn: Yes, many will perceive her to possess a boy's name, but this doesn't bother her for Shaugn is a contented soul who is replete with life, laughter and nous, and who views the world as a peculiarly wonderful place that needs to be experienced to the full.

Shauna: Potentially lush and exotic, Shauna is actually arid and complex like an expensive garden bed that hasn't been given enough water, and which is slightly frustrated that it hasn't.

Shay: See Shae.

♀ FEMALE

Shaz: The Queen of the Roadhouse.

Shazza: Shazza uses modern day metro-sexual men to wipe her arse.

Sheba: Big. Black. Beautiful.

Sheena: Like any adult female Killer Whale, Sheena is gentle and intelligent on the surface but there is an inner strength that has to be seen to be believed.

Sheila: You might think that Sheila is dangerously dumb but you'd be a fool if you did. Apart from being possibly red-headed and buxom, Sheila never misses a trick.

Shella: Shella always seems to be in a rush but despite being either a little bit basic or maybe a little naive, she's a nice person.

Shelly: Energetic and never dull, Shelly exists in the same way as an extremely hot curry: In the short term she's a bit too much but in the long term she's tremendous and/ or perfect.

Sheridan: Sheridan over-thinks it, she over-does it, and she is therefore problematic.

Sherie: A more unglamorous version of Cherie, although her mood swings aren't as catastrophic.

Sheryl: As Cheryl's older cousin with much longer hair, Sheryl copes a little easier with life and laughs a bit more. And she's far more musical.

Shiloh: Shiloh is a tonic to sadness or anger. What you do is say her name three times whenever you feel yourself begin to 'lose it': *Shiloh....Shiloh.....Shiloh*, you intone. Mysteriously, all the anger, the fear and the frustration that you felt will begin to abate, leaving you feeling content and happy. Loving, even. (Alternatively, of course, you could just go around to her place for a cup of tea.)

Shiralee: Shiralee is a loaded metal spring that is quite rusted. If she doesn't shoot straight when she goes off, and she usually can't, then you can expect to receive some kind of nasty pinch on the skin, or possibly even a nice rusted cut.

Shirl: It's mid-January, Longreach, Queensland. You've pulled up at a servo where you're prepared to pay $5 for each litre of diesel you're about to fill your Landcruiser with, and Shirl comes out to greet you in a old pair of blue shorts with matching blue shirt, a rough and ready smile and sun-blasted frizzy hair. "How are ya'?"

Shirley: Self-deprecating and wholly loving, Shirley dreams of the day when she is paid for taking bubble baths. She loves the suds, you see. When she's tipsy, she throws them in the air with her hands and yells, "Yippeeee! Bubbles!"

Shona: Shona packs a mean, all-knowing and sexually-charged punch.

♀ FEMALE

Sienna: A sexy Italian city. (Twice every summer the locals have a horse race around the main piazza that's filled with a million people, and they yell and scream while the riders try to kill each other. When it's over and won, everybody parties for two days, hugging and kissing anyone else who is moving or relevant, and then wonder what the hell happened. I'm not sure if there is a rehab clinic nearby but they probably need one.)

Sierra: Famous for her white bikini and her huge dark sunglasses, Sierra is beautiful and frivolous.

Sigourney: Her single-mindedness seems to intimidate everyone but there's really no need. Sigourney cool. Everyone, say hello to her. She won't bite. She's nice.

Silvana: "All the boys,
think she's a spy....."

Silvia: See Sylvia.

Simmo: Simmo wears a short skirt and runs the two-up betting ring at the Broome Cup, where she gets to party hard and yell at the top of her voice. She's hard to miss.

Simone: A legal secretary that dresses in drab colours. She loves American TV dramas and, secretly, she thinks she would have done well on Big Brother.

Siobhan: (Pron. She-bonn). See Kiki, except that her dad might be part Chinese.

Sissy: Foxy, in the good old fashioned way.

Sky: Sky sunbakes in the nude and is learning to be a naturopath, karmic healer and transcendental therapist. She has no idea who or what the P.M is but she makes up for it by being smart in ways that us mere mortals have no idea about.

Skye: See Sky, although Skye knows who the PM is. The trade off is that she isn't nearly as skilled at seeing the future.

Smiddy: Smiddy gets shit done and she makes others laugh, and she's got that *thing* about her that drives men crazy. Yep, she's hard to miss.

Sokina: Many people, these days, have Asian words tattooed on some part of their body as a symbol. They speak of things like 'peace', 'love', 'happiness' and 'fertility'. "Sokina" is what a young girl in Tokyo, for example, might tattoo on herself to reflect a similar idea: the letters (symbol) looks nonsensical yet inviting, and deep down you know that, somehow, it represents mysterious greatness.

Sonia: Sonia rhymes with 'Hurry up'. Like any female spider worth her salt, if Sonia is ever pestered, bothered or let down by a man in her life, she will immediately deem him to be of inferiority quality before clinically dispatching him. She will then feast on his body at her leisure.

Sonya: Sonya may or may not have a Macedonian grandfather, in which case the gloves are off, but like her slightly more reactive cousin, above, she is a sensual woman with full comprehension of who she is and her place in the world. She is definitely someone worth knowing and loving, platonically or otherwise.

♀ FEMALE

Sophia: Remember this: every perfect mango that you ever eat for the rest of your life is not just a mango – her name is Sophia. Please don't forget it.

Sophie: Your favourite block of chocolate. (As a quick aside, her name in your mouth is a quaint and hot little blob of sweet tasting glue that bonds her to her good friends very strongly, and she's only too sweet about 14% of the time.)

Spider: Great value and 'out there', Spider is a big wholesome country girl who drinks a lot of piss.

Stacey: Stacey is a very neat and perfectly functioning stapler and it's not possible to run an organized and professional looking office without at least one of them. (Unless she's the Stacey that races motorcars and says, "I fucken hate pre-menstrual bitches", quite often.)

Stef: She's your mate, good friend, bosom buddy and pal. She rushes into the pub/house/studio in a fit of being late in lieu of some remarkable disaster that could have only happened to her, but that's okay. She's here now, so let's get our coats off and get on with it.

Stella: The tired old battle-axe who, no matter how much the roof leaks and no matter how hungry she gets, is always able to find something to laugh about.

Stephanie: Everything's fine, then you start pedalling up the hill when all of a sudden your chain comes off. "Oh no!" you yell. "I've had a Stephanie!"
Invariably, you swear and curse as you wrestle the chain back onto the cogs, ending up with grease all over you, but if you stood back and analysed the situation rationally you'd see that you were only off your bike for about 40 seconds. And, truth be known, you enjoyed standing for a few moments and stretching your legs, didn't you?

Stevie: A cross between Isaac, Bec, and a female Smiddy, Stevie throws herself into the world with abject gusto. Some days she wins, some she loses, but as a hopeless romantic she always expects greatness to arrive in the next couple of seconds.

Stretch: All the girls envy her long legs – all the boys want to kiss them – but behind her physical attributes is an intelligent and sensitive soul who, like her male counterpart, might not be as laconic as her name suggests.

Sudha: Like a specially wrapped dark liqueur Swiss chocolate, Sudha is unusual, round and delicious.

Sue: Sue is the sort of woman that will buy a rabbit infested shithole of a property and spend the next 40 years transforming it into an award winning example of re-claiming of native lands, of reforestation and of environmentalism. Thankyou Sue.

Su-lin: A beautiful, understated and sensual woman who, at a moment's notice, can propel an argument through a brick wall.

Summer: Broome in August; Byron around Easter for the Blues Festival; Lorne for Falls – these are some of the places you might find her, for Summer is an noncommittal breeze of sweet smelling pollen. I've no idea what will happen to her – or how she would cope – if the country falls into a deep depression. She might just disappear into thin air and wait for the good times to return.

Sunitra: Sunitra is the name of a gorgeous tigress living undisturbed in a Sumatran jungle. She's so beautiful and aloof that most men seem inexorably attracted to the notion of catching her and putting her in a box. Not a good idea gentlemen....

♀ FEMALE

Sunny: Unusual. Sensual. Charasmatic.
Question: Is she a Top 10 Enigma?
Answer: If you can find her, you will know the answer.

Susan: The first daughter born and a born fighter, with it. Susan can be extremely uptight, and her name is impossible to say with a smile on your face. Like a good tomato plant, therefore, Susan will always benefit from plenty of light and summer sunshine.

Susanna: Interesting. If she was taught the piano on a Grand Piano as a child then forget it, she's a goner. But if she learned to drink and dance at nightclubs way before her 18th birthday, look out, because in that case she is one of the Gifted Ones; Magnetic, funny, incredible...... all that.

Susanne: Susanne qualified for her MENSA membership at the age of 11 and as an adult she now concerns herself with dealing with the rights and wrongs of the world. (The legal profession is full of them.)

Suzanne: Rather ironically, Suzanne is highly skilled in the art of reclining on a banana lounge while wearing a tastefully revealing bikini, and while a cabana boy brings her a cocktail.

Suze: She might be a little slippery for some and, apart from all the other sexy-funny-good stuff, she's read a million books.

Suzi: Suzi is polished, exotic, sensual and exciting, not to mention as sharp as a tack.

Suzy: See Suzi, basically, except that Suzy is ever so slightly more responsible. I wonder what happens at a party when a Suzy meets a Suzi?

Suzy J: Botanist. Rainforest ecologist. Dynamite.

Suzzan: A nice helpful lass who works at the Post Office.

Svetlana: Crazy Eyes.

Sylvia: Sylvia is one of the world's more capable women. She doesn't tolerate too much shit from anyone, she has an innate desire to actively live her life and not just sit around, and amid all this she gets on with the business of loving and nurturing her family and friends. Time isn't something that she has ever wasted.

Syreeta: (English). She loves her nails and her dress sense. She hates lizards, bugs, spiders, snakes, sharks, sea urchins, jellyfish, cows, trees and grass.

Tabitha: Tabitha is a small furry mammal. She is nocturnal and hunts small rodents that, like her, prowl the forest floor in search of food. If you try to pick her up when she's awake you will receive nasty bites and scratches to your hands and cheeks.

Tabrett: Tabrett loves visiting casinos in a slinky dress. Especially when there are a heap of doting men around who are happy to buy all of her drinks.

Tahlia: The name of any pair of rubber dishwashing gloves that are extremely snug, initially, until you realize that they're so tight that they're cutting off the circulation to your fingers. Your palms may also sweat tremendously.

Tahnee: A total fruitcake.

Talei: Another innocent girl whose mother thought that all actresses must have weird names.

♀ FEMALE

Tam: If she isn't a bit unusual like a Tim Tam that's been dropped in the dirt – and therefore kind of enticing in a not-very-nice kind of way – then Tam is that sexy girl that every man always thinks of as mostly a friend, until it gets to midnight on New Year's Eve. At that point they tend to see the truth: that is, that she's gorgeous, normal, funny and charismatic, and definitely someone worth falling for.

Tamara: Tamara rhymes with 'Get out of the Way'.
You'll often see her bursting out of a flame-filled house covered in soot, grime and perspiration, with an axe in one hand and a child in the other. She's won so many bravery awards it isn't funny. She keeps them on a shelf in the toilet.

Tammy: The name of a beautiful soft blanket that you wrap yourself in on a cold night before slouching on the couch for a bit of TV. The only thing you have to watch out for is a single large hole about as big as a basketball and, depending on where it is located, you may be forced to wrestle with a chilly breeze on a part of your body that will make it difficult to relax for very long. So, can you see the hole?

Tamsin: A type of knot used on boats. They're excellent in foul weather but impossible to undo.

Tan: Tan leans across a smoke-filled bar at two in the morning, with a fag in her hand, a sneaky smirk stuck to her face and a recently emptied shot glass in front of her. She's smiling increasingly at some ridiculous story that a drunken friend is telling her, about some other twit who did something stupid, before she pipes up. "Oh yeah," she drones, "…like one of those beige bastards."

Tania: What you see is what you get. Tania is a sexy and vivacious girl, by and large, who is always surprised at how well her hair salon is going.

Tanya: The genial mortgage broker.

Tara: Tara inhabits a body from the Gods and lives in the ancient city of Atlantis. She wears a thin white gown that is partially see-through and everyone wants to hang out with her – be they man or woman.

Tarahnee: The name of that exquisitely beautiful pang of pain you get in your throat after sculling a full glass of Salvital* when you're dying of thirst. God, she's good....
*. A fizzy saline drink that you gulp down when it is maximally bubbling.

Tarni: The raging bull who is as cute as a button.

Tarryn: Often sexy and invariably complex, her name is surprisingly vacant, not to mention very Darren-like. As such, the ghost of a chip-on-her-shoulder lurks in the background.

Tash: Tash is an energetic and sensual being whose main goal in life is fun-seeking, but there's more to her than that. Her relaxed nature is welcomed by everyone although she will gladly hurl herself into the action if prompted by love, hate or need.
(Note: The blonde-Tash is more irreverent than the brunette-Tash, not to mention more common, although this is probably a function of men giving more attention to blondes and thus allowing them more space to be silly, basically.)

Taylor: Taylor is a tall, let's-not-fuck-around bombshell.

♀ FEMALE

Tayu: Shiny black hair. Dark humorous eyes. What mysteries lie behind them? How will her tiny frame cope with the world? What great deeds are yet to be done? And great deeds, it seems, are what's in store.....

Taz: As a set of shark's jaws in a natural history museum, Taz is exotic and fascinating but pick the jaws up in your hands and you'll tell a different story; the teeth are so sharp you won't even know you are being cut. So, friends and lovers, bring gloves, expect the unexpected and take your time.

Teagan: Check-out chick.

Teen: Teen is unique in the Kingdom in that she isn't really an Enigma, and she isn't really one of the Gifted Ones. She is, however, some combination of the two in that her name rhymes with Comfortable and it rhymes with Yes. The trade-off for her is that she wears her foibles on her sleeve and for that she receives our thanks, our envy and not to mention our unshakeable love.

Teha: Teha is a nice girl but a stiff breeze, be it real or analogous, would blow her over.

Tehya: See Teha.

Tenille: Witchy and pinny.

Teresa: I don't know if it still happens today but back in the old days you used to put Teresa in with the shirts to make them stiff and white. Does that still happen?

Terri: (One of) the Gods gave her that name in the same way that insurance companies give you a cover note between cars. That is, Terri is relaxing in this life while she is between two highly energetic universes, and so what she was called while she was here was always going to be irrelevant.

Terri is her name, and Terri gets on with it: end of story.

Tess: Take note: that hard-arse bitch exterior is just a bullshit front. Be patient, take your time, ignore the quips and go discover someone quite lovely and peculiar. Go on...

Tessa: The patient lioness.

Thea: The sensuous looking prickle bush.

Thommo: The delectable woman who occasionally suffers at the hands of a manly nickname, making her sound less sensitive and feminine than she actually is. As a trade-off she's shit-hot when the chips are down and sufficiently gorgeous and lovely, anyway.

Tia: Tia is fun and glorious on the surface until you get her angry, or you get her on an off-day, then she'll bare her teeth like an unpredictable Ridgeback.

Tiaani: With a name that resembles a $15,000 pearl necklace, Tiaani is either as sweet, as relaxed and as playful as can be, or she's the other extreme of the egocentric cow who has her head buried so far up her own arse that it isn't funny.

♀ FEMALE

Tiate: Tiate is spritely and generally lovely, but she looks so far ahead she's nearly cumbersome to deal with in the here-and-now.

Tiech: As a teacher, of sorts, Tiech is the social, advisory and entertainment hub for all of her friends, of which there are many. She'd be okay without them but they'd be screwed without her.

Tiff: Lively, playful and light-hearted, Tiff doesn't easily display her anger.

Tiffany: Tiffany plays the bangles in any rock band and she has a big hairdo. Tell her she's a gifted artist and she'll be your friend forever.

Tilly: Tilly wears glasses and she's abit scatty. She's sweet as pie until she gets catty.

Tina: The Tina is the act of ripping off a bandaid that's been on the back of your leg for ages, and she is the whole journey; the psyching up, the fear of the pain, the pain of the rip and the blessed relief that arrives afterwards when you discover that the wound has healed nicely.

T'meya: "Give it to me," she says, placating the person that matters with a luxurious kiss on the cheek. "....What? Who do you think I am, you blue collar scum? When was the last time you heard of anyone mixing tomato sauce with their beluga?"

Toby: Toby is like the Energizer battery bunny on TV ads because she never gives up, except that she's far more alluring and definitely not a fuckwit.

Toni: Toni heads to where she is going on one of the most direct routes possible. Her tomboy heritage made her that way, but it didn't quell her sense of fun or adventure. Don't ever assume that.

Tonia: Whippet-like. Tonia is one of the most organised and antsy people in the Kingdom. Every ounce of her soul is busy continually preparing for *something*, such that if she is feeling cocky, she might even attempt to schedule the timing of her visits to the loo, for the following day.

Tony: The gorgeous, the brilliant and the incredibly ambitious lawyer. Just watch her go....

Tonya: See Tonia.

Toorah: The in-your-face actress/adventurer/soothsayer who tends to blow people away.

Tori: "....Why make something simple when I can freak out and let it ruin my life? Tell me, why? Why would I do that? Make my life simple, I mean....why? Who needs a simple life, anyway?".....etc etc.

Trace: A fart in a country pub: generally unnoticed and often funny, she's a splendid reminder of those things that make each of us splendidly human.

Tracey: The professional tennis player who is far more skilled at the game when she's warming up: She has an excellent scowl on her forehead that you know isn't all that serious, she looks fantastic and very professional in her tennis skirt and her technique at hitting a pretend ball is dramatic and flawless. When the actual game begins, however, her shots start flying everywhere and I don't think she's won a Grand Slam event, yet. But, she tries very hard and for this we must be, and are, very thankful.

♀ FEMALE

Tram: Tram is special because she seems to have
all
the
time

in
the
world.

Trin: Like a magnet, she attracts men, women and all other energetic entities. (It's all that spinning, that does it.)

Trina: She'll never make CEO of Rio Tinto but she's a highly energetic woman who manages to be quite economical at the same time.

Trinity: Trinity rhymes with Uppity.

Trish: Trish is a laid back larrikin who deals with danger in her stride, until the cruise liner that she's travelling on, via the competition she won, hits something and begins to sink, and sink quite quickly. Then she screams as much as she laughs.

Trisha: The textbook Drama Queen.

Trudy: Trudy is a bit rudy. She's had an eventful upbringing but, overall, she's compensated with poise.

Tuhi: Tuhi's ancestors used to paddle around New Zealand in canoes and eat any visitors that showed up, and she has lost none of that zest for life. As Maoris go, Tuhi is a gem but the standard warnings apply to her as to all Kiwis: If she is pissed or partying hard, either call the police or hop in your car and leave for a couple of days (unless, of course, you want to see something spectacular, in which case I'd recommend sticking around).

Twiggy: Sexy, funny, loud and impossible to keep up with.

Tzena: Aggressively proactive, Tzena is a beautiful woman who thinks and acts with her heart.

Uma: Archaeologist. The last time anyone saw her she was in Peru where she was leading an expedition into a giant Inca temple only recently discovered in the jungle, but that was years ago.

Ursula: A myth. A fable. No woman, *no person*, is ever this sexy. (With the exception of Susanna, Daniella and Isabella etc.)

V: V is misunderstood and intense, possibly obsessive, and usually lovely. People are sucked-in by the ease and quickness of her name when they think that she is a relaxed persona for this is rarely the truth.

V2:   The rocket ship that tears off in some general direction. Has she landed yet? If so, was there any damage?

Val: The name of any vehicle that has crossed the top of Australia and is now covered in a 3millimetre layer of red pindan. The trip was hard and long but, by God, it was fun.

Valeria: A gorgeous and sensitive woman. End of story.

Valerie: Valerie is on her last life and she is doing okay. However, she is a middle-class worry-wart.

Vanessa: The quintessential corporate woman.

Vegas: Spectacular.

♀ FEMALE

Vera: So long as she's comfortable in her clothes Vera doesn't care what she looks like. She loves all cheeses, detests all children and in a past life she was a sturdy curtain rail.

Verity: <u>Option A:</u> Verity has an intricate and geometrically perfect haircut, her spectacles match her handbag and she has a beautiful speaking voice.

<u>Option B:</u> Tartare sauce: To be served with cold fish, shellfish and cold vegetables. Keep in the refrigerator until needed.

Veronica: Veronica wears a layered petticoat under her skirt and the spectacles on her face aren't dissimilar in style to those worn by Dame Edna Everage.

Vettie: Vettie Biscetti. She's got heaps of scrapes and scars on her legs and knees because she runs full tilt into the guns, all the time, dragging whoever she can, kicking and screaming with her (even though they secretly love it, and need to be dragged).

Vic: The super-chilled out Victoria. The ego and all the hype is still there, which is a good thing, but she won't kick you under the dinner table if you mention to the assembled group of how out-of-it she got the other night, and what she did afterwards.

Vick: This girl is as comfortable with herself and the world as anyone and 95% of the time, at least, she cruises along with a quietly determined air, as if life is all too easy. Yet, why does it feel like something is still missing?....

Vicki: Highly intelligent and picky, 'V' hates the fact that every second person spells her name wrong.

Vicky: See Vicki.

Victoria: Victoria is the name of a big, beautiful mare. Her chestnut coat has a glorious lustre and she stands before you proud, glistening and powerful. However, how close you get to her will be up to her, and her alone. She may deem you worthy of little more than a kick in the face; then again she may let you run your hands through her glorious mane with only love on her mind. Who the hell knows but good luck!

Vida: The effusive control freak – which means that there's a good chance she's South African. She drinks a ton of coffee.

Violet: The angel that watches over all of us. She's thousands of years old, has a deity-like wisdom, and can't understand why everyone seems so stressed, angry and depressed these days.

Virginia: Virginia is a chilled-out lady who, at 60 years of age, still looks amazing in a ball gown or a bikini. She has tons of friends (like Denise, Jackie and Pam) and when they get together at the cafe every Thursday morning, without fail, they talk so much that no one nearby is able to hear themselves think.

Viv: There aren't many words that can be said in the course of normal relaxed breathing – Viv is one of them. Her name, therefore, rhymes with Yes, Sure, Anytime, Not a problem, If you like, If I like, Whatever you want, Whatever she wants and Whatever you feel like. And what does that all mean? That Viv is cool and interested, and possibly pretty sexy.

♀ FEMALE

Vivian: "Viv - i - an".....rhymes with..... "On - her - own." She lives in Fitzroy, in Melbourne, and spent a long time getting over a heroin habit that has enabled her, at least, to experience the spiritual world in ways that she never knew possible. Now that she's clean, she runs her own business that sells crystals and aromatic oils. There's a psychic out the back on Tuesdays.

Voula: Sensual and determined, as a businesswoman with a Greek heritage Voula loves it when her work life, her family life and the general bullshit we all have to deal with form a collective bed of screaming, hilarious chaos.

Wendy: Like a shower that seems to have a personality all to itself, Wendy is scattered, lively and occasionally awkward.

Whitney: Whitney was spoilt as a child and this had dire ramifications later in life.

Willa: To describe her as rare is to say nothing. Her name is competently off the ground and gliding like very few others, although there is more to it than that. She might even be the world's first female Dalai Lama. Let's just watch and wait....

Willie: The classical airs and graces of a polite feminie lady are absolutely none of her business.

Willora: Like a rip old egg-laden salmon not long for this world, Willora's aspirations are pretty simple and she moves through life like the aforementioned fish swimming steadily upstream to spawn. Barring catastrophe she'll get there.

Willow: Zany, crazy, hyperactive and dangerous? I don't think so. Willow, like the tree, is thoughtful, unusual, curvy and genuine.

Wilson: She walks with her eyes pointing down like a criminal, her thumbs inside the sleeves of her jumper, and she rarely shaves her pubic hair. The last I heard she was off to the U.S for a huge meeting of girls.

Win: Her Vietnamese heritage assists her but as one of the most agile and nimble decision makers in the Kingdom, Win always gets what she wants.

Xiindi: Highly energetic like a sexy little buzz-beetle, Xiindi is musical and worldly, as well as perfectly peculiar.

Yalda: You say her name and you want to scream out, then you stop, and you listen. 'Yalda,' you say again. 'Yes,' she says, and you have nothing more to add because you know the truth. Yalda is here – here she is – and she is lovely.

Yasmin: Yasmin wears buckets of perfume and glossy red lipstick, sometimes a black head-band, and she has large eyes that look startled most of the time – as if she is a newly born gazelle just learning how to walk.

Yasmine: Yasmine has time and she has style. She reads other peoples' body language as if holding an expensive vase with a pair of fine white gloves, and she hardly ever flashes her knickers.

Yelena: Seductive. Inquisitive. Intriguing.

Yolanda: A strange ghost with dark hair.

♀ FEMALE

Yve: If only we could make a movie of what Yve gets up to on the weekend because at 6pm every Friday, two sexy little horns appear on her head, making her all the more delicious and remarkable than she already is.

Yvette: The news journalist for the ABC. For the past few months she's worn a flak jacket every day and can often be seen on the 7 o'clock news where she submits regular reports from Bagdad. She recently quit cigarette smoking and she's not very happy about it.

Yvonne: Self-sacrificing and loving.

Zali: Refreshing and upbeat like a freshly squeezed fruit juice that has a heap of ginger in it, Zali is healthy, different and enlivening.

Zenda: The director of a reputable and compassionate funeral service company.

Zenela: Zenela is the name of a drive in the country with a couple of friend's friends, who turned up two days ago and are now struggling to find something to do. (You read the bible, they do drugs and strange sex acts, or vice versa.)

Zeva: The sensual and worldly non-pushover.

Zita: As a kitchen Bamix she looks cool and curvy, even though she doesn't do much until she is stimulated into action in some way. If that happens then either stand back or take care.

Zoe: When she's not a princess-in-waiting, she's a princess-proper. Everyone flippantly assumes she is conceited and arrogant but they'd never tell her because, deep down, if they stopped and thought about it, they'd know that this is untrue and that this news would kill her if she ever found out. Zoe is never that nasty.

Zsusanna: Zsusanna knows things about Lawrence that his wife has no idea about.

MALE

MALE

*"I wonder why men get serious at all.
They have this delicate, long thing
hanging outside their bodies which
goes up and down by its own will. If
I were a man I would always be
laughing at myself."*

Yoko Ono.

Aaron: A conniving little shit that squeals like a piglet if he doesn't get what he wants. When he loses a game of badminton, for example, he'll often belt the victor in the face with his racquet.

Adam: Adam is a perfectly weighted chunk of granite that sails through the air in a lovely parabolic arc before making a wonderful ba-doink noise as it enters the water. Adam.

Aden: As an open and thoughtful individual, Aden deals with responsibility very well and the only real serious trade-off is that, in a million years, he'd never suddenly reappear sleep-walking in the nude at the dying end of a big dinner party, having gone to bed early because he had to work the next morning.

Adrian: As a potential control freak, his name is the first thing you say after trying on a pair of shoes that are a size and a half too small. "Oh, ouch!" you yelp as you stand up, "No, their Adrian's."

Agron: Agron rides a dragon to work so it makes sense that he's a bit strange.

Aiden: The name of an icebreaker ploughing steadily through the frozen waters of the Antarctic. He is safe and ultra-reliable in even the worst weather.

Adie: An irreverent soul who wants to be where the action is. Whether he turns out to be a tortured artist or not, he is a sensitive, giving guy who has a lot of love for the world.

Ag: An exact male version of his female counterpart, and she's marvellous.

♂ MALE

Agro: Named after a furry puppet, Agro doesn't have an evil bone in his body and, instead, is impressively quick-witted.

Al: Al is alert, he's hardly ever alarmed and, baby-face or not, he might even be a rather relaxed genius....

Alan: The local butcher.

Alastair: Alastair feels that he'd be best suited for an amicable coupling with someone who is aesthetically, financially and morally superior.

Albert: A comedic legend that rarely exercises. Having said that, he's surprisingly quick on his feet, he loves a joke and he's young at heart.

Alby: Alby rhymes with "Naah, she'll be right, and if it breaks, well.....fuck it....it's not ours anyway."

Alec: A high-powered name on one level but, basically, Alec is too nice to be ruthless and apart from being embarrassed if you ever suggested he should be, he has to carry around the mantle of 'what might have been'.

Alex: Not a scratch on his female counterpart. The 'x' at the end of his name is like a cross road where he stands for most of the time unable to make a decision.

Alexander: Alexander married his colleague, Lily, and boy don't they have fun? Fortunately they have no close neighbours.

Alfred: Alfred is a quiet old man who wears a Panama hat but no one knows that his younger years were spent exploring the rivers or Northern Africa. He has lived quite a remarkable life.

Alfy: There are probably a million irresponsible larrikins in the world and here is another one. The further north in Australia Alfy originates from the more fun he is and, regardless of how much work he doesn't do, he is impossible not to like.

Ali: Think long hair. Think calm in a crisis (and possibly so calm he's useless). Think reserved of opinion.

Allister: Accountant.

Ally: Mummy's favourite.

Alvin: Alvin was turned into a frog by an evil witch but he's quite relaxed about it now. He looks like he's smiling all the time and, like many good frogs, he pisses distilled water, which is great fun at parties.

Alwyn: The gifted, mysterious and mischievous garden gnome.

Ando: The Fork Lift.

Andre: He speaks Spanish – or at least everyone thinks he does – and girls love him, but for some reason he never seems to *look like* an 'Andre'.

Andreas: Andreas approaches the various aspects, tasks and components of his life like a dedicated scientist that leaves nothing to chance. This very driven nature can be painful to deal with, let alone observe, but he has a good heart and he's probably good at chess.

Andrew: I don't get it either because nearly all Andrews are decent people, often wonderful, but it's a nothing name that doesn't actually do anything at all. The best we can say is that he might be a quiet mystery. At worst, a nothing bit of nothing.

MALE

Andy: Similar to his cousin, above, his name drops away into nowhere right at the end when it needs to fly and he therefore spends a lot of time feeling slightly disappointed. But, he's not half as bland as he sounds because he is a generous and friendly personality and the only question we have is, can he prevail?

Angelo: Upbeat and opportunistic.

Anglus: The axis of any rotating sphere. Every moon, planet and star has one, and they are constant forces in a silent universe, which means that some are more perfectly hidden than others.

Angus: Devoid of any fanfare, Angus is contented and always well prepared. If you want to fix a situation then get him over immediately. Don't speak to him unless spoken to, and if he asks you to do something then do it without question. It'll be the right thing to do and it might very well save your life. (If you are married to one, or intend to, don't expect him to remember your birthday.)

Anthony: Anthony hates it when he's called Tony but it happens so often that he lets it slide, although this does build up a slight, if not general, resentment of the twits that he's surrounded by. Normally, he holds a PhD in either physics, law or some kind of biological science.

Antoine: Antoine drives a 40 tonne truck at a mine-site up in the Pilbara......(just kidding).
Antoine is a bar of soap and he smells nice.

Anton: As a mild-mannered physician, his name isn't short for anything and it isn't long for anything. Indeed, it's just right. Anton.

Antony: The temperamental coffee maker with a Southern European heritage who talks non-stop. He's rude to most people, he loves to dance close with beautiful women in the same fashion that a large fake Coca-Cola bottle rotates on a milk bar counter, and he loves his own reflection.

Argo: To call Argo a loner is to assume he is only happy in his own company, and this isn't so. Argo is one of the very few gifted geniuses, and defining genius, on any level, is effectively an exercise in artistic appreciation. Argo loves people just as he loves life, but he is able to throw his thoughts and imaginings so far from where he stands that not many are able to grasp what he capable of, or where his mind is. In short, Argo is crystal-pure, and unique to the point of distraction.

Ari: His entire name is off the ground like an Osprey at full tilt and this boy, therefore, can do just about anything and make it look pretty easy. In which case, he needs our congratulations.

Ark: Take a breath, now hold it in. Hold it.
Don't breath, and listen.

Listen to the stillness. Listen...
Can you hear it?

...Ark.
That's him - the noise of perfect nothing. No one knows how he does it.

Arnold: A rare South American nut that is very hard, albeit delicious. It's so hard in fact, that if you dropped it from the top of a very tall building onto a bitumen road, it wouldn't register that anything has actually happened to it.

♂ MALE

Art: Yes, by default he possesses the temperament of an artist, but he is also The Quiet and Remarkable Achiever.

Arthur: You might think he's a dour old man, but he is, in fact, a funny bastard who has lost his keys. He knew he put them down *somewhere* but for life of him he doesn't remember where. And he's late. Naturally, he talks to himself while he searches in the hope that some Lost Key God will find humour in his search and thus show him where they are.
This is Arthur's lot.

Ash: Ash is beautiful, flexible and contented like one of those monster trees that live in The Valley of the Giants, in Western Australia.

Ashley: A good-looking smart arse. He and Dean are as thick as thieves, and they occasionally are.

Ashton: The Flat Football.

Asif: Asif endeavours to plan most things metic-ulously.

Aubrey: Aubrey got whacked in the nuts playing cricket as a kid and gave up sport immediately. Today he designs tax breaks for corporations and hangs out with Christian, Jonathon and Benjamin.

Aussie: A Kiwi. Except he moves like a Sloth and ingests way too many substances.

Austin: Austin is the name of a fat gold ring that's worn on the pinkie of a fat man who is middle aged, wealthy, and in the process of discovering his homosexuality.

Bailey: The fat happy man that giggles constantly. He works for a merchant bank in downtown Sydney and apparently he's pretty good at what he does. Often seen with spittle on his shirt of a Friday night, all he wants from his life is to hang out with his friends and try to talk to girls.

Bairdy: It is alleged by chemists, physicists and modern-day philosophers that inside Galaxy Bairdy, the normal laws of Quantum Mechanics do not apply. Indeed, they *cannot* apply.

Baker: Tough nut. Funny cunt. Good value.

Barnaby: Barnaby loves it when one of his mates has a buck's party because it means he can try and kiss the strippers.

Barney: The name of any man who owns and runs a pub.

Barrie: The Gentle Giant.

Barry: Barry is a genial fellow who is rarely rushed and whose heart in the right place.

Bart: Basic.

Basil: How can one scientifically describe a beautiful painting? Should we? How? I mean, where do you start, especially if it's an abstract piece? Take the colours for example.....they're *supposed* to be strange and comedic, right?

Bastian: Reasonably forthright and conscientious, Bastian is a traditional man. So traditional, in fact, that he pines for the day when terrorists wipe out the power grid so he will be able to meet and greet foreign and exotic women via the use of an introductory letter that has been written by someone else. (Who knows? Maybe he's a budding terrorist, himself?)

♂ MALE

Baz: The 'zed' at the end of his name bubbles like French champagne (or VB) and so whoever he is, Baz is effervescent and outgoing in some way, and probably more than most of his peers.

Beardy: He has a beard and he is a gifted maniac.

Beau: Beau rhymes with "Oooh!"
It is also the name given to the phenomenon of a bag of banana lollies being carried by a 4 year old, who then drops the bag, which splits, sending the bananas sprawling through the sand. In anyone's language this is a tragic event.

Beecher: Like a possum preparing for winter, if Beecher sets out to do something he generally does it.

Ben: Deep in a shallow kind of way, Ben inhabits the role of a loner more than you might think. He may not be the life of the party although he's not always predictable, either, and he'd definitely suffer at the hands of an interrogator for longer than most.

Benjamin: Benjamin is a neat, nice and formal individual without being a pain about it, hopefully, and yes, he's a mild soul that appreciates the good in the world. We can't all be John Travolta.

Benji: As a North Sea Viking in a past life, Benji is full of Scottish blood and rollicking good humour, although these days he is *so* nice that even he admits that girls with large bosoms frighten him.

Benny: Cheesy.

Bernard: As a patron of the arts and a patron of all things related to the delivery of humour and life, Bernard loves champagne and his friends and he's a marvellous person to have around, but don't waste his time by asking him to fix your car.

Bernie: Bernie is the sort of man who, at formal functions, will curse at his reflection in the men's toilet when he realizes that, three minutes earlier, he was chatting-up a girl while he had flecks of food stuck to the side of his chin and an unusual globular shaped mass inside his right nostril.

Bert: Midway between a fart, a burp and a bump in the night, Bert is a light-hearted man who makes everyone feel eminently comfortable – special, even. I wonder where he has gone....

Bevan: As a close relative of Eugene and Nigel, Bevan is absolutely more energetic and intelligent than one might presume. The great side-effect of the comedy of his name is that he has more friends than most people, and he's always pretty busy.

Bill: Sometimes a handshake is all you need to tell you that you like a person. This handshake is known as The Bill. It is a rare and wonderful event.

Billy: Billy perfected his graffiti tag about six months ago and this week, having been given a dare in front of a girl that he really likes, he plans to ride from Werribee to Melbourne on the top of a train. There's a 19% chance that he'll live to tell the tale.

♂ MALE

B.J: B.J plays hard (at least he did as a young man), he works hard, he loves his friends and family and he has a very deep sense of what's wrong and right with the world. And he'll do what he can to help.

Bjorn: A breath of fresh air.

Blackie: Betwixt between the intellectual world and the soulful realm of the undercurrents, Blackie is sort of bloke who is truly at peace on his surfboard. He just gets it, and in more ways than most of us will ever understand. He's not an ornithologist, for instance, but he can spot a New Holland Honeyeater quicker than anyone, although, as a trade-off, he carries a whip-like temper.

Blair: He's no bar-room brawler, but Blair *is* intensely ambitious.

Blake: An ego-fed American name for a normal sort of Australian bloke. Is he a tosser? Let's hope not...

Blue: Shy around girls if he hasn't got a beer in his hand.

Boaks: An affable bloke who rarely rushes things, and who learns from his mistakes.

Bob: Bob is a Kingswood ute that's done about a million miles and he has a fair bit left in him yet. He's not in mint condition and he's not meant to be. (Good mates with Graeme.)

Booker: Booker is the kind of bloke who submits a $9million boat plan to a boat-building company on white butchers' paper, having spent five minutes drawing it with a black crayon.

Brad: If he isn't a new yo-yo (ie. a fad that comes and goes without affecting the philosophy of those that he mingles with) then Brad is a calming soul whose direction in life seems to have been perfectly predestined. It helps that he is almost invariably tall, but in this case, even a short conversation with Brad is enough to provide you with clarity of insight.

Bradley: Honestly, does anyone really care?

Brady: Brady is a nice enough guy and, yadda yadda yadda, but he's completely inoffensive.

Brandon: Brandon is the branch of a gum tree that broke off in a storm about three years ago. He was sturdy and flexible when he hit the ground but the months in the summer heat have dried him clean and made him frail. Nowadays he'd make easy prey for a hot summer fire that was gathering steam and he'd snap in your hands if you tried to break him in half, but there's a 20% chance that, if you did that, he would slap you in the face as the final energetic act of his quite complex life.

Braveheart: Big, loud, bold and red-headed.

Brayden: Born into a nice middle-class family, Brayden is good in school, popular with people, successful in life and happy. True, he won't ever trek to the North Pole, discover a new species of fish in Lake Victoria or get 'Hi, how are you?' tattooed down the length of his member, but he'll procure a wife, have three kids and enjoy watching them grow, and contribute, just as he did.

Brendan: Like any sensitive concrete block, Brendan is functional, surprisingly conservative and occasionally highly competitive. And he's nearly always tall.

MALE

Brent: Organised. Preoccupied. Occasionally intolerant. Possibly shy.

Brenton: Brenton is about as charismatic and endearing as a dry thicket fence.

Brett: The universal gods were mucking around in the kitchen one day and they put John, Shane and Nathan in a blender and vwa-la: Brett.

Bretto: The Remarkable Clown.

Brian: The lemon tree in the back yard that is pissed-on by dogs, men and children. He doesn't produce tonnes of fruit but he's growing in excellent soil and it is therefore no effort for him to produce more than enough lemons of the highest quality.

Bristle: Bristle is a Commando or SAS soldier and adrenalin is the only thing that makes him tick. On at least one occasion, for example, he has leapt from an aircraft with an Alsatian strapped to his chest.

Brock: Brock would make love to his reflection if he could and he can be extremely impatient.

Brody: Brody the Show Pony. For employment he works as a bell on a little girl's new bicycle, unless he's the Brody that cuts down trees for a living, in which case he's far more elemental and genuine – good value, as a matter of fact.

Brooksy: The Camel. He's his own man, he hardly ever feels the need to rush, he sleeps whenever the need takes him, and for as long as he likes, and if he's feeling social he is excellent company.

Browny: Like an exposed Kimberley escarpment that is 200 million years old, Browny is true to the bone.

Bruce: Bruce rhymes with Clunk. As an anvil in an iron monger's workshop, Bruce has been whacked and hammered with all forms of hammers and mallets but he's up to it. It gives him something to belt his head against, and there's no harder crunching in the world than metal banging against metal.

Bruno: Bruno, we're trying to sleep here so can you just shut-up?

Brutus: Remarkable for not only his size and strength, Brutus is famous because he can be easily convinced that, by placing each foot in a metal pale and gripping the respective handles in each hand, if he tries hard enough, he can actually lift himself off the ground.

Bryce: If the day comes when the American President has to get on the TV and tell the world of a meteor that has been discovered hurtling through the universe on a trajectory that will make it catastrophically collide with Earth, then he or she will read from a prepared statement that those in the White House know of as the Bryce Statement. It will be well articulated and perfectly presented with emotion, compassion and hopefully a drop of humour, but in the end it's all about telling us how we are going to die. It's probably a nice way to be told, truth be known.

Brycie: You grin when you say his name and you therefore smirk when you think of him, so it's probably a given that you laugh and be grateful in his company. Brycie is a cracking bastard, all round.

MALE

Bryn: Bryn is a cross between a grin, a surfboard fin and a big fat bunger as rolled by a happy hippy.

Buck: ....you're joking, right?

Buddha: Buddha is lucid and completely real.

Buddy: Dangerous and brilliant, Buddy is the mercurial wonder child. Let's just pray he never gets to grow up....

Buggy: Like a frustrated Border collie who wished that his owner would just throw the fucking ball, Buggy is fun-loving, highly intelligent and direct.

Bullfrog: Bullfrog has big red chubby cheeks and probably carries the tattoo of a lily on the point of his shoulder.

Bumhead: A bit thin on top.

Burkey: You could spend years writing a thesis about Burkey and who has the time for that? Suffice to say they made one cast out of bronze and never replicated it. Not once. Its name is Burky and he can do anything.

Burt: See Bert.

Bus: His name says it all. He sports a large welcoming personality and he loves to travel, although if he stays in one place for too long grass tends to grow-up around his wheels and he ends up never leaving.

Buzzard: Tight-arse.

Cadel: Like a fighter pilot with his thumb hovering over the trigger, Cadel is calm and primed but....does he *believe*?

Cale: Cale is another country boy who grew up swimming in channels and rivers, as well as getting pissed and shat on by the cows in the diary shed at 4 in the morning. His success in the arena of romance was largely achieved by pure luck, but he rides that like everything else and these days he does quite nicely, walking a straight line to those things he covets – utes, Crownies, new boots.

Callum: Big ego. Maybe too big.

Cam: Cam is a tremendous fellow. Relaxed with an edge, he understands women and men, he knows who he is and, most importantly, as a never-say-die optimist he endeavours to like everything.

Cameron: Cameron is a deep thinking man – deciding how to put out the garbage on a Monday night sometimes requires an intricate analysis, for instance – but the sad fact of the matter is that Cameron, the word, looks and sounds like something that a youth might extract from his or her nose. "Bloody hell!" Clint might say to Billy one afternoon, after they've robbed a defenceless grandmother and left her lying in the street. "Check out *this* Cameron!"

Campbell: As a rather formal and boring secondary school college made of old red bricks, all Campbell wants to do is leave some kind of legacy.

Carl: The brand new livestock fence. His posts are new and chemically treated, they are exactly perpendicular to the ground and he sports new grade 9 fencing wire. He is tough to get passed in a hurry, however, and often you have to think long and hard about even attempting it because he usually has 240 volts running through him.

♂ MALE

Casey: Casey is perfectly contained and concentrated, and while his decisions aren't always well thought out, when he decides to act he moves like grease lightning.

Cecil: If he isn't at least 75 years old, Cecil is weasely and limp-wristed.

Cedric: Cedric is an Australian dairy farmer that speaks so quickly everyone assumes he's telling one long undecipherable joke, which is both lucky and tragic because he's bloody funny. Much to the lament of his wife, however, Cedric is absolutely useless in bed.

Chad: The boating, diving, fishing type. If he isn't one of those, or he isn't physically active in some significant way, then his ego takes over such that he becomes a grossly overconfident bore.

Chance: Chance is streamlined and highly skilled at whatever he does, and luck has very little to do with it.

Charles: The starfish that lives on the bottom of the ocean. He moves slower than anybody and he can regenerate a limb if it is eaten – it's a slow process, after all. Charles may not be the first person you'd invite to the New Years Eve party at the Playboy Mansion but at least he doesn't drink much.

Charlie: Nick with an education.

Chaz: The flamboyant Italian who made good. His daughters are gorgeous but woe-betide any man he catches looking at them for too long.

Ché: With a spirit that is stripped and pure to the core, Ché lives in the moment. He understands how good and bad deeds procure the future in very different ways, although he struggles to reconcile the notion that it is nigh impossible to have one without the other.

Chito: If modern society ever regresses back into Roman times by allowing the major television networks to produce a game show whereby people win prizes by killing other people, then Chito will be a world champion at dispatching others with a spear from surprisingly large distances.

Chongo: Mr Disco at night. Plastic surgeon during the day. Like the Great Monkey (of Pigsy, Sandy and Master, fame) Chongo is world famous and irrepressible.

Chops: Doesn't and/or can't shut-up.

Chris: Chris is far more complicated than his female counterpart. As a mole that lives in the ground, he lives a neat, organised and dignified life that, on an outrageous day, could nearly be described as mysterious. Ensure that you don't mess up the entrance to his burrow, however, because he's liable to get quite angry.

Christian: Christian either reads too much of the Bible or snorts too much cocaine. Perhaps both.

Christopher: Teased by the boys at school for his lack of sporting prowess, he got his own back when he took over daddy's multinational. And that's all wonderful, but no one knows that every Thursday night he sneaks a quick look over his shoulder before he steps through a dark doorway of a dingy little bar in Kings Cross that caters for just about anything. There had to be a reaction sometime.

♂ MALE

Chum: Chum attacks life like a lion attacking a gazelle, except there's never any harm or malice in his method because all he's really trying to do is encourage the gazelle to rejoice in its life so much that it begins to radiate light. Personal motto: Have disco, will travel.

Clarence: Clarence has a huge lung capacity and a very low resting pulse. He is therefore quiet and peace-loving 99.2% of the time. (Note: Just beware of the remaining 0.8%.)

Clarky: Mr. Irreverant. Clarky will tell you that if you want to go and do something (eg. surfing, mud-crabbing, cafe building) then you should probably just go and do it.

Claude: Without doubt Claude is the laziest person on earth. He drags his feet when he walks and he lives for breakfast in bed.

Clay: Maximally alert, he ain't, but Clay is definitely solid.

Clem: The farmer with the old man's soul. The climate is heating up, which isn't going to make his life any easier, but he also knows that there's no point being too glum about it either.

Cliff: Cliff has a dry sense of humour. It is so dry that he might be considered incredibly cynical.

Clifford: If he isn't a wonderful traditional Australian artist, then he is a pompous boring white-fella that lives in his pompous boring white-fella mansion. Ironic, eh?

Clint: His name is a cross between a clit and a c_nt, and while we can thank a male dominated world and the various quarters of most (male dominated) religions for the negative connotations of the latter, Clint is the one who has to wear it. He might be intelligent, fast-moving and determined, but in a subconscious attempt to prove he's not a c_nt (or a clit), there is a high probability that Clint is actually a complete wanker.

Clinton: By default, Clinton is upright and diligent but this is only one facet of this rather unique organism. His name sounds like it has been poured into a mould of perfect conformity and efficient management, and it's so formal, in fact, that he has actually passed out the other end of that spectrum to become one of the world's great eccentrics.

Clive: Clive is so clumsy that, on average, he falls over three times every week. But, generally speaking, because he appreciates the world as being one of the funniest things he's ever heard of, more often than not when he does fall over he'll remain on the ground for some time afterwards laughing at his own self. It's a beautiful thing.

Clynt: (Man, that was close.) Clynt treats most situations in life as some kind of lottery prize and he is therefore rather gifted and enigmatic.

Clynton: The name of a Picasso painting that recently sold at auction for $112 million. How did that happen??

Cobey: Liar, liar, pants on fire!

♂ MALE

Cody: Affable and cosy to deal with, Cody is well positioned to use this empathy for his own ends, which he occasionally does, either deliberately or subconsciously. (Having said all that, he might be incredibly boring.)

Col: The tall and slightly out of shape middle-aged bouncer, who works at the pub every Sunday afternoon. He'll kick people out if he has to, and he can handle himself, but overall all he wants to do is see that the young kiddies have a good time without hurting either themselves or anyone else. His home life is actually very sedate.

Colin: Colin nearly disappeared during WWI because all of them were used as cannon-fodder by the British Army. As fate would have it, he now grows the best roses in the world.

Collins: A good panel-beater who actually thinks better when he's underwater.

Con: A survivor.

Connor: See Bradley, unless he has a genuine Scot heritage, in which case he's a funny, rambunctious bastard.

Conrad: A powerful man who, as a means to show that he *really isn't* infertile, loves nothing more than travelling to far-away lands and slaying as many natives as possible in the name of progress.

Cooper: Cooper drives a late model BMW and spends a fortune on clothes and dry cleaning bills. He subscribes to the Financial Review and he ensures he leaves a copy in the front seat of his car but, aside from his these macho fantasies, he's alright.

Coops: The Harley mechanic who, like any devoted artist, lives and breathes his passion. If he ever fell asleep across his chopper with his shirt off, you'd be hard pressed to discern the paintings on his body from the paintings on his bike.

Corby: Careful in life. Watchful with money.

Corey: See Cory.

Corrin: Corrin possesses more male beauty products than almost any other non-female in the Kingdom. Facial scrubs, cleansers, anti-wrinkle crap – you name it. He has the softest hands in the world.

Cory: The wet slice of bread.

Coskun: A perky little fellow.

Courtney: More feminine than his female counterpart, Courtney is about as useful as a tub of margarine that has been left outside near the barby, overnight, and is now a partially melted lump with all manner of crumbs and meat clippings caked all over it.

Coxy: Coxy is a charismatic man who has a multitude of dodgy contacts, not to mention a sprinkle of even dodgier vices.

Crackers: A supremely unflappable lunatic.

Craig: A complex mathematical equation. The solution, of which, will assist us in understanding how the universe is going to evolve. IBM's Deep Blue supercomputer had a crack at it, once upon a time, but it suffered a meltdown and no one has been game to tackle it since. I wonder what the solution is...

♂ MALE

Crash: Difficult to ignore, Crash is an impressive individual who is anything but demure.

Crocket: Crocket has his hand on it, but he takes it as it comes and he does most things in his life pretty easily, as a result.

Crutchy: Nuggetty.

Curly: As an aboriginal in a past life and a gifted artist in this one, he is a seeker of truth whose passions live on his sleeve. Make of that what you will, but love drips out of his pores like the sweat of a beautiful black man that has just walked into the Derby pub, having left Broome about three days ago in the middle of the wet.
(Note: If asked about the state of his phallus, he will reply that he is in possession of an "evil cock".)

Curtis: Curtis possesses a highly acute acumen and he promises much.

Cyril: Cyril lives alone with his dog up in the hills, he brews his own liquor and he shoots rabbits that they both share. Sometimes he cooks them, sometimes he doesn't.

Daf: See Dafydd, except that this one seems to make more sense.

Dafydd: Dafydd has been compelled to turn into a complete weirdo – his Welsh heritage probably helps. He is never glum and no one knows if he has ever had a job, aside from professional skateboard rider for a while, and we only assume that because he rides one everywhere, trailing a mop of crazy hair, or what he has left of it, and possibly a line of giggling children.

Dale: A small mountain lake. Calm on the surface and freezing cold, he is so deep and inviting that no one actually knows how deep he really is.

Dallas: The singer Sade sang a song about him: "Smooth operator, smooth…..operator." (In theory)

Damian: Damian is extremely single-minded. If he is a rational man then he is capable of great things but if he isn't, and 65% of them aren't, then he might be so blinkered that he is potentially dangerous. The only great one is a vascular surgeon who wears a chic black leather jacket, so technically they're not all bad – even though it was a typically 'Damian's' intelligence and drive that got him there in the first place.

Damo: Nothing like his painful brother, Damo is a sensitive, funny and kind-hearted bloke who lives the physical male life; pearl farming, mining, tuna fishing, etc etc. Well-suited to the Australian summer, they are nearly always blonde.

Damon: A perfectly-weighted name for a well-weighted man, and whose core stability precludes almost all irrationality. In short, Damon is rock solid, intelligent, different and funny, and absolutely nothing gets passed him.

Dan: The all-round Mr Nice Guy that mothers and grandmothers pinch on the cheek and say, "Oooh, you're such a beautiful boy!" He now coaches a boys' basketball team and wears a cap everywhere he goes.

Dane: Blessed with a calm head and an imposing persona, Dane times everything to perfection.

♂ MALE

Daniel: A clever and gentle-natured man at his core, Daniel is the last person you'd want next to you in a life-and-death situation and the last I heard he was answering telephones in the customer service department for most of the major banks. But, Daniel does carry a morbid edge sometimes – a secret garden, if you will.

Danny: Moody. He feeds an inferiority complex by drinking too much and he has friends on the surface but, in truth, most of them feel sorry for him.

Danté: Hardwired to Satan.

Darcy: Corrin is the champion, no question, but Darcy does alright in the bathroom department. Other than that, he's a good guy with plenty of friends, and who expects to do quite well.

Darren: Darren is a brickies labourer, which is handy with a booming property market, although women are no good to him unless he can root 'em.

Darryl: Completely unrelated to his rather plain step-brother below, Darryl is the debonair devil in sheep's clothing.

Daryl: Nutritious and uncomplicated like a decent-sized potato.

Dav: Dav gets straight to it with a no-nonsense attitude that he somehow melds with a knack for keeping it real and light-hearted.

Dave: Dave is a light-weight dead-end, which is why everyone feels like they know him and why people feel immediately comfortable around him. If he isn't saved by some other nickname then he needs to be barked at by a drill sergeant; "Stand up straight boy! Don't slouch! Get some ambition in your life!".....that kind of thing.

Davey: Quixotic.

David: The heavy D's at both ends weigh his name down like the legs of a Bass Straight Oil platform, and to this end he may be too deep and sensitive for his own good. However, the 'V' in the middle provides a powerful launch pad for virtually anything. We wish him well.

Davo: A big ball of coloured play-dough used by children under the age of 5.

Dazza: Dazza does his best work at the Bachelor and Spinsters' ball in the hours between 2am and 6am, such that people have no choice but to take notice of him.

Dean: Dean works at an abattoir where he operates a machine that kills cows by the hundreds. He eats lots of steak.

Deano: The free-thinking shit-stirrer. When life is good he's there, front and centre. When it's bad, you won't see him for dust because he'll be off somewhere else, trying to make it better.

Declan: Heralding from the same blood line as Sasha, Declan enjoys the luxury of being indulged by others, and he subsequently nearly always gets what he wants because people expect him to be himself.

Dekka: Big, gentle and unconventional.

Dempster: Charismatic and unusual, Dempster is a dark horse in nearly every category.

Dennis: Not exactly a rogue elephant, Dennis is more like a rogue daffodil, with the occasional exception of Dennis the Alcoholic.

Derek: Faced with a room in which pandemonium reigns – people yelling and swearing, sobbing in some quarters, plates breaking, music blaring, tempers flared and emotions high – he will wander over to the cupboard, open the door peacefully, wait for silence to settle and ask, "Would anyone else like some cashews?"

Dermott: The name of the physiological process whereby something is rolled into a sphere by peristaltic movements and the associated secretions of mucous. A fur ball spat out by any cat is a classic example. (Unless he's the Irish Dermott, in which case he's a semi-talented stand-up comedian.)

Des: Des is the name of a dust-covered Rolls Royce motorcar that's been sitting in an uncle's garage for nearly 20 years. No one is certain, of course, but there is a popular perception that if he was ever to wake from his slumber he would be a marvellous and reliable individual.

Desmond: Like his dog, the poor boy is just a bit slow.

Despot: "Hey," he says, on the morning of the 25th, hungover from the night before, and ready to go again. "Merry Christmas....fucking!"

Dick: The informal name hides the formal nature of the fellow. Mr. Cool, Mr. Deceptively Competitive and Mr. Genuine Nice Guy, he is. And he has a sense of humour. (It's the only obvious part about him.)

Dicka: A normal fellow (he isn't) who is in possession of a rapier wit. There were rumours that he once wore loud shirts and sported a short mans' syndrome, but this theory has been subsequently debunked.

Diesel: Detached and inert when he needs to be, and sometimes when even when he doesn't, Diesel is one of the most determined individuals in the entire Kingdom.

Digby: Digby has huge ears like Babaar the elephant. They turn red when he gets excited and if he's really excited they start flapping.

Dimce: A pesky little bastard with a lightning sense of humour who can multi-task better than most men. He's always on the look-out.

Dimitri: Dimitri's first reaction to people he doesn't know is one of utter warmth.

Dingo: Another Kiwi (what are they doing here?). His idea of the perfect meal is a special kind of slop that involves making a soup of mash potato containing at least one can of carnation milk, into which are dropped two or three lamb chops that have been incinerated to within an inch of their lives. Like his personality as a whole, the entire thing is borderline-carcinogenic.

Dion: The IT guy.

Dirk: Dirk is the only man in the animal kingdom who has willingly super-glued both of his hands to his own cock.

Dirt: Trailer trash.

Django: Drummer.

Dominic: Dominic is passionate to the point of being lethal. He's the sort of man, who, if he took to the back of a horse for the first time whilst in love, and enraptured with the moment in general, may very well ride the animal to its death.

♂ MALE

Doc: Doc is super smart and possesses a photographic memory but he has very little common sense.

Don: A council worker's shovel. He holds a lot of dirt and doesn't mind grovelling in mud one iota. In fact he enjoys it.

Donald: Donald is a donkey that lives in Egypt. He walks slowly, whether he's carrying much weight or not, and he doesn't understand why something like the pyramids generates all the fuss that they do.

Doone: Doone is a fascinating creature. Over time he has evolved special receptors in his brain that have attuned his senses to the movements of rock within the earth's crust, which is only one of his many eccentricities.

Doug: The name of the great moose head that's hanging on the wall. He's great to talk to when you come home, pissed as a mute.

Dougal: (No description needed.)
Everybody....I'd like you to meet Dougal!

Dream: Originally from Nepal and originally named Nitten Redicum Bak Bak, Dream is the sort of fellow, who, when standing in the light of a roaring bonfire, rolling a cigarette and quietly swaying to music of the party, will elicit a sudden and instinctive scream of, "DREEEEEEEEEAAM!!", from the two desperados sitting down, nearby, who have simultaneously spotted him, and who have given up any hope of finding anybody with a lighter. We're lucky to have him.

Drew: Thoughtful. Quiet. Measured.

D.S: The hidden artist. D.S is constructed of splendid moral fibre that enables him to exercise his substantial talents. From the ground, up, he is designed perfectly for whatever it is that he decides to do with his life.

Duane: Duane presents very little, although he does excel at church group.

Duck: Wet feet.

Dudley: A comic genius who doesn't know it. He still can't understand why the Queen gave him an Order of Australia but he forgot all that nonsense when he rushed-off to try and rescue the love of his life. Bravo Dudley! Bravo!!

Dummy: Alright, so he doesn't have a clue how long it takes for photons of light to travel from the Sun to planet Earth, he has the table manners of a frothing pig and he's never heard of Bolivia, let alone its capital city, but Dummy is a bona fide legend. Why? Because he is a lover and a fighter who susses people out in a flash – be they good, bad or useless – he always thinks laterally, he is a generous friend and when it comes to women, he is a gracious gentlemen.

Duncan: Option A: The Solemn Priest. He is at home in front of his brethren. He is at home on the ocean.

Option B: The name of Sean's cock.

Dundee: Dundee used to work at the croc park and he has almost certainly slept with Deidre.

Dunny: Salt of the Earth.

Dustin: Polite and reliable, Dustin does a good job of cleaning up the edges.

♂ MALE

Dutchy: Maybe he's from Holland. Maybe he isn't. It doesn't matter. In the same vein as Clarky, Bill, Joe, Graeme, Jack, Jimmy and Bob, Dutchy is here for the stay, for the good times and the bad, he'll laugh and help when he can, if he can, and in the wash-up all of us are glad that he is around. And when he's gone we will mourn his absence. Cheers Dutchy.

Dylan: Like the rubber grip of a handle for anything that has a handle, Dylan looks okay and provides *something* for the universe, but most people aren't bothered by him, one way or the other.

Eamon: The name of a particular colour of paint. He's not black, he's not grey and he's not blue - he's Eamon, and he pleasantly fills background space without tearing the room to pieces.

Earl: Earl loves rugby league, lives for ten pin bowling with his mates every Friday night and he is a gifted football hooligan. He wears lots of rings.

Early: Early has clear head and he doesn't talk shit. He may have had a tough start to life but it has made him tough and true at the finish.

Ed: Closely related to Malcolm, Ed is a huge log that you throw on the fire in the dead of winter. He is a massive awkward thing that takes a while to lumber into place but once he gets going he throws out enough steadying light, heat and humour to warm all but the biggest of rooms. (Serendipity is his close ally.)

Eddie: Full of wisecracks and hair-brain schemes.

Eddy: See Eddie.

Eden: Eden is one of the Gifted Ones in that he is perfectly centred, he is innovative and he carries a glorious sense of fun. He'd make a good father.

Edgar: A nice thick piece of cheddar cheese. Pregnant women sometimes crave his company and he often forms the part of many-a-meal that might be described as 'comfort food'.

Edmund: (Walter's younger cousin.) Edmund says, "Yes dear", "No dear", "Sorry dear" and, "Okay dear", so often that he sometimes says them in his sleep.
Poor Edmund.

Edward: Edward always wears spectacles. As a leading diplomat in the foreign office, he spends most of his time placating visiting V.I.Ps who are still offended by the behaviour of some of his embassy staff at the party that was held the night before.

Einar: His parents were Swedish politicians, which is one thing, but no one has any idea how to either spell or pronounce his name. The only thing we know for certain is that Einar rhymes with "When do you think your gonna'?", and to that end he charges at life like a drunk village idiot in a bad mood. Get in his way and you're basically fucked.

Eko: A cross between a gecko, a rainforest and an extroverted hairdresser, Eko and his Indonesian heritage are the perfect example of compassion, good grace and cheeky clean fun.

Eli: Graceful, musical and unflustered.

♂ MALE

Elliott: An upstanding man who doesn't take things too seriously, and overall he's excellent company. Aside from being highly intelligent, Elliott is also the name of a musical note that's played on a flute by a man wearing tights.

Elvis: When all the other parties have petered out on a Friday or Saturday night, everyone heads back to Elvis's pad and to the one party that will ride it out to the dawn, and possibly the one after.

Enrique: In Spain he might as well be called Shane – who knows – but here, he's a potent ball of energy that, like several of his peers, lives for the sight of girls' knickers. And he generally gets to see plenty.

Eric: Eric is a light-hearted Goat and one of the Gifted Ones in that he is the luckiest being in the entire Kingdom. Outstanding effort, Eric.

Ernest: The name of an old country homestead that sits on a rich pastoralist's property. Quiet, calm and cool in the heat of the summer, he battens down the hatches in winter and hibernates.

Ernie: '......and he drove the fastest milk cart in the west.' Enough said, although he probably doesn't have any eyebrows.

Errol: A Fiat Bambino 500 motorcar. Forget Herbie the Clint, Errol has style and panache, and he makes others laugh by simply looking at him.

Ethan: "Eee – than" rhymes with "Not – fair". As a serious young man who lacks the ability to grow any kind of facial hair, the only avenue for Ethan to look older, therefore, is to frown constantly. But, he's okay.

Eugene: For an unusual name Eugene is just a normal sort of bloke, and a nice one. (Note: The thing about Eugene is that, though his name begins oddly, it quite quickly becomes an unexpectedly smooth ride over rolling green hills.)

Evan: It doesn't happen much these days because the world's gone to CDs and beyond but once upon a time vinyl records were all the rage and sometimes they received scratches, and every time the needle ran over one it would skip. "Evan...Evan...Evan..," the speakers would blurt, and you'd drop your head at another album destroyed.

Ewan: You can't help but contort the inside of your throat to say it, but somehow he manages to pull-off a great comeback. Regardless of that, Ewan is a nice guy and a skilled carpenter who is as good with his hands as he is with his repartee.

Ezra: His hair is curly because he is sufficiently electrifying, hence I would advise not getting too close to him if there's a lightning storm overhead, and you are either wet or standing on some kind of metal. He's a great fire twirler.

Fab: See Fabio, except that but you'd be wrong to think that Fab isn't an intelligent or thoughtful individual. And he's more creative than he lets on.

Fabian: A flittering-nothing-fable of a character, who kind of wanders around aimlessly like a ghost with current-existence issues.

Fabio: Fabulous Fabio is a big guy with an Italian heritage and a big ego. He works out at the gym a fair bit and he's proud of the result. And...ahh...yep.....he's proud of the result.

♂ MALE

Fatboy: Eat a dick.

Fazio: Fazio is a social butterfly that sticks to the pubs, clubs and cafes near the beach. He is a shit hot dancer and carries a permanent erection.

Felix: The loveable and gifted bank robber

Fenn: A cross between a still Irish glen, an ancient Otway fern and a Tasmanian pig pen at feeding time, Fenn is both tranquil and ridiculous.

Fergus: His IQ score is in the top 0.5% of the population, which explains why he's so fast with the perfect one-liner. Apart from being very funny, Fergus is one of the true sexual deviants.

Fetch: A doer and provider of services and goods.

Finchy: The lone policeman in a small country town. Everyone knows his name and nearly everyone respects him as a decent bloke who is doing a good job by doing the best he can, while at the same time always giving people the benefit of the doubt.

Finn: Having arrived at the last of his reincarnations, Finn is not far from the finish line and it makes sense then that he is a placid and ostensibly good individual. None of us are going to feel like having a full-on party at the end, anyway.

Fish: Completely unrelated to his female counterpart, Fish is extremely lucky, and he's English. He drinks hard, he plays harder, and after he left the army he wound up working for a Sheik in Saudi Arabia. No one knows what he does, and he'd be hard pressed to explain it himself.

Fitzy: Redneck.

Fizzipoodle: Loves reading highly detailed maps.

Fletch: Fletch is so laid back that he hardly gets anything done. He is, however, arguably the calmest person in the Kingdom in that he never panics, ever, and the last breath of air that he takes before leaving this life will be used to tell some kind of joke.

Flint: The disappearing act. We're sure he's good fun but no one ever seems to know where he is.

Floyd: The buffoon with good looks – albeit, a buffoon with a rousing sense of humour because, not only does he know he's a buffoon, he actually goes out of his way to tell others he's a buffoon.

Foxy: At some point in his life Foxy will exactly resemble the four-legged variety and much of that guile has carried over because he is a wonderful and enigmatic smart arse, who'll only end up in the rubbish if his girlfriend kicks him out of the house for being drunk.

Francis: The Sicilian tomato farmer who migrated to Australia in the 60's and grew lots of white chest hair. His original name was Luigi but he changed it after he arrived so he would fit in, and he has one of the strongest handshake grips in the world.

Frank: One of the world's generous men. Regardless of that, Frank can speak for quite a while without actually saying very much.

♂ MALE

Frankie: Frankie is the name of the bloke who sells hotdogs out the front of the disco after it shuts. He loves pretty young girls and he loves hotdogs with onion, mustard and lots of tomato sauce, but get him drunk and you might see a different fellow, altogether – possibly a dangerous and crazy one.

Franky: The Lighthouse.

Fraser: Whether he has a chip on his shoulder or not, Fraser has huge reserves of energy that compel him to live a busy life. And he'll never back down from a fight, even if he is bleeding badly.

Fred: A 1200 year old Huon pine that lies undisturbed in a secluded section of the western Tasmanian wilderness. Some woodchoppers saw him once, years ago, and elected to leave him be and to this day he casts a loving eye over his beloved forest. He has survived generations of howling gales from the roaring forties, and he never gets tired of celebrating his life by closing his eyes and swaying in a warm afternoon breeze.

Freddy: The name of the bloke that runs the meat tray raffle at the footy club, every Saturday night.

Frederick: Frederick is a Swedish backpacker living some-where between Bondi Beach and Port Douglas. He is just over 6 feet tall, has blonde eyebrows and is kind of skinny.

Frog: Frog is another all-round nice guy, and the most we can say about his capacity to save world is that he is here.

Fuck off ya': Covered in tattoos, Fuck off ya' C_nt is an enthusiastic man who spends most of his spare time on the seedier beaches of Thailand and the Philippines. Irrespective of that he is a smart guy who, like many in the Kingdom, carries a beating heart made of gold.

Gabe: An energetic, kind and busy young man who darts about the world with a strange kind of athletic elegance.

Gabriel: A serious fellow with brooding looks and dark hair.

Gæton: Well-travelled, artistic, educated and competitive – be it in the kitchen or as a downhill skier – Gæton tends to live large.

Garret: Calm. At peace. Garret is the kind of man who, as a lone father, would have no reservations at taking his two young children on a three month tour of India.

Garreth: Garreth is purposeful with a giant intellect. If the undertow of his ego doesn't suck him out to sea then he is capable of absolute greatness. If it does, however, he'll be a complete tosser.

Garrick: A likely lad who believes that life is short.

Garry: There's a red wine stain on the lounge room carpet that he left one night after he turned up drunk and unannounced.

Gary: See Garry, although this one is less predictable and far more light-hearted.

Garth: As a pick-up line to a girl, he'll say, "......umm...do you wanna' go outside....and umm....check out your pool?"
And by the end of saying it he is visibly wincing at how pathetic it sounds.

Gator: Gator doesn't live in Sydney or Melbourne as he's better suited to a much warmer clime. This doesn't stop him from planning well, however, and he therefore tends to do things properly, wasting no or little energy in the process.

♂ MALE

Gavin: Elemental. Gavin is genuine and ostensibly tranquil.

Gav: He's either a large dopey bloke from Darwin that watches a heap of TV and puts away at least a six pack a night, or an eccentric gay hairdresser from Tasmania. Both are equally fun and dangerous on their day.

Ged: (Pron. with a hard G) Ged is indestructible, paradoxical, sarcastic and sufficiently enigmatic.

Geoffrey: The Evil Uncle.

Geoff: Regardless if he owns a construction company or is involved in the conservation movement, this fellow is basically rock-solid with the odd sprinkle of greatness at the edges. (He is unique in the car world for his renowned reliability.)

George: Plonk goes the dollop of cream on top of the apple pie.

Georgie: Never without a multitude of friends, Georgie is a big kid at heart who, at the tender age of 55, is liable to have a very young wife.

Gerald: A lovely old fellow that lives on his own and plays the piano in the nude.

Gerard: As a young man he was once kicked out of a nightclub for trying to sneak into the girl's toilet and watch one of them take a pee, but not long after that he discovered God and became determined to cleanse himself of such damnations. Today, as a man of the cloth, he often wears a funny white gown and speaks in dramatic tones with his hands held in the air, in the same way that a doctor walks into an operating theatre having just washed them. Very odd.

170

Gerry: Gerry is not as outlandish as one might think. He walks with an easy gait and he has the capacity to marvel at the tiny things as well as the large. At his core he is a calm and searching soul who listens and observes, offering advice only when asked or if a situation or person obviously requires it.

Giacomo: Giacomo stands on the deck of his Spanish Galleon with a wench in one hand and a telescope in the other, searching the horizon for any generally irresponsible mischief to be had.

Gianni: Enthusiastic. 8 out of 10. Occasionally 8 and a half.

Gib: Smooth. Gib doesn't mess around with useless deeds or thoughts and he only falls to pieces if kept inside for too long, where there is a good chance he will suddenly turn into some kind of caged animal. He'd die if he had to spend a winter in Sweden or Finland, although, having said that, he'd probably satiate his sense of adventure by stealing away with a pack of huskies and a dog sled where he'd quite happily feast on raw venison until he got bored with the lack of girls to chase – or be chased by.

Gibbo: Option A: A big, beer drinking, chauvinistic Queenslander.

Option B: The name of a colourful old blanket that is tossed over the back of a donkey in a Spaghetti Western. As such, he's an ideal contact if you intend to carry guns or tequila.

Gideon: Musician, artist, hippy, philosopher, grave digger or glass blower: this is where you will find him.

♂ MALE

Gidz: Gidz is a cynical, if not a very humorous individual. If watching an ad on TV that he detests, he will leap to his feet and swear that he'll never buy that product again. And he never will.

Gilly: As a Japanese girl in past life he has a fetish for Asian Kung-Fu movies. Gilly rhymes with 'Hii-yaaaa!!!', after all. And he's one of the few people on earth whose smile is actually wider than their face, which aids him to be one of the world's truly generous men.

Gimp: The Gimp loves burrowing down inside his hole and meditating. In a good mood he ponders things like love and the synchronicity of the universe. In a bad one he licks his lips and conjures up notions of perfect evil.

Giulio: A preposterous galoot.

Glen: Glen is like the state of California in that he is affluent, good company (generally) and occasionally 'out there', but through the middle of him runs something akin to the San Andreas fault. The question is, when and/or will the entire state suddenly tear apart and slip into the Pacific Ocean? Who knows.....maybe it won't?

Glenn: Glenn is alright but his parents are completely dyslexic.

Googie: Googie is a light-hearted soul who doesn't actively decide anything at all. Years ago he read a book called The Dice Man, and in allowing 'the universe' to dictate how his life unfolds, it has never been the same since. God only knows what he's up to today...

Gordon: Gordon is a big personality and a great hulk of a man in body and/or spirit. He's rollicking fun at dinner parties, for instance, until he gets pissed and tries to lift up all the girls' skirts.

Goughie: Goughie rhymes with, 'Jesus, that was close..', as well as, 'Anyone seen the remote?'
Overall, Goughie gets on with life in a no-nonsense fashion, cruising with the luck that he seems to generate himself, and his approach has paid off because the result is a contented bloke who is more than happy to put on his girlfriends' bathers at a moment's notice.

Graco: Probably too intelligent for his own good. Graco is extremely charismatic and he does play games, although he only does it to give himself something to do because most people bore him, shitless.

Graeme: Graeme is like water. In the driest continent on Earth, therefore, he is an iconic figure because he provides energy and life without any fanfare. I'm not sure where any of us would be without him.

Graham: Graham is basically the same as his brother, but he isn't as good at getting his hands dirty.

Grant: Grant is potent and single-minded. He's often misread as a bully or a grouch but that's not right – he's just doing what it takes.

Gratias: Gratias is as quiet as a mouse until he gets pissed with the boys.

Gregory: Gregory died out in the early 80's when the ozone layer started to disappear. It was probably a blessing.

Greg: Plain like a pancake without anything on it. Greg is so plain, in fact, that he is occasionally very bitter about his own boring normalness.

Greig: The aloof stalker.

♂ **MALE**

Guppy: No hidden tricks here, folks. Guppy plays pretty hard, he begrudgingly works pretty hard, and all in all he's worth his due.

Gus: Gus was a roo shooter for years until he discovered how much he enjoyed being at sea, and where he truly discovered the effects of gravity and momentum. The last I heard he was driving fishing boats out of Port Lincoln but he's always been good with engines.

Guy: 17 yrs old no matter how old he is, Guy has a terrible time trying to explain why and how a 41 year old man has as many wet dreams as he does. In life, his decisions are often rash and he's a hopeless lover, but it's not all bad because he's one of the few men that has the capacity to autofellate.

H: Lonestar.

Hal: Hal rhymes with Have As Much Fun As Is Reasonably Possible, Think About What You Want and Understand The Consequences Of Your Actions. In short, Hal is a wonderful old sage whose name and presence opens people up.

Hamish: A reliable and kind-hearted fellow who doesn't beat around the bush despite being raised there. "Are you talking to me?" he asks with complete sincerity. "What do you want?"
He will then give your response 100% of his attention.

Hank: The name of the filthy fat man who is driving the tow-truck that comes to rescue you in a dodgy part of town at 3 o'clock in the morning. You can smell his body odour before he gets out of the truck, which in itself is bad for the environment, and he is one of the most splendid visions you have ever seen in your life.

MALE ♂

Haren: Haren is a wonderful and quirky little fellow who fossicks about with some kind of constant smile on his face, like he is about to engage in something so ridiculously fun and childishly stupid that he can barely contain himself.

Haris: Succinct in dealings and emotionless to those who don't know him, Haris exists as a reminder that nothing in life is straightforward.

Harley: Harley is light on his feet and he'd make an excellent thief, rapper or kick-boxer.

Harold: Harold wears full pyjamas to bed every night and tries to sit very straight whenever he eats. It's good for the digestive system.

Harris: Film expert. Wears a beret.

Harrison: You poor bugger.....your mother was so enamoured with the Star War's and Indiana Jones' character that you're now carrying the mantle. As a walking cliché I suggest you change your name and give yourself a break. You're a nice bloke, so what about Bill? Have you thought about that?

Harry: Jocular.

Harvey: A well maintained, sufficiently lubricated and perfectly functioning gearbox of a Kenworth truck. He works when he needs to work and he laughs loudly when he wants to laugh loudly. Why wouldn't you.

Haset: Haset is so full of family love that he is almost exploding. Beyond that, picture Dot in a male body.

♂ MALE

Hayden: ….as opposed to Hey Me, or Hey Look. He sometimes tries to stick his chest out all day long and he's a broken man if it turns out that he doesn't have one. (Alternately, if he was named because his mother once drove passed Hayden Bunton Rd, in Perth, Hayden is an outstanding person.)

Heath: Unpredictable. You don't want to meet Heath in a dark alley in a rage.

Henry: "Good old Henry," you say. He's not bright enough to be evil but he's certainly good enough to be wonderful. And by God, he is.

Herb: Herb is the sort of bloke that walks back into the farmhouse at the end of another stiflingly hot day, having spent most of it shooting the sheep on his property that were starving to death in lieu of the drought that has devastated his land and his livelihood, and still has a smile for his wife and kids.

Herbie: Paedophile.

Hercules: As an ex-God he's allowed a few liberties – and he takes them, which is fair enough – but no one ought to get used to resting on their laurels. Doors don't just magically open these days, chief.

Hilman: Completely honourable, upstanding and polite.

Hinze: Born in Hamburg, Germany, Hinze is now 62 years old and is the chief curator at a rock museum.

Hocko: The sort of bloke that gets so out of it, one night, he accidentally does a shit on the floor at the end of the bed, while at the same time uncontrollably pissing on the beautiful woman who happens to be sleeping on it. Nice work Hocko.

Holden: Pimp.

Hollywood: Hollywood loves to flaunt it and people are sick of telling him to put it away.

Howard: Howard is a saturated log that's lying on the bottom of a river, or maybe a lake.
Question: What's he doing?
Answer : Not much.

Hoang: The little boy racer with a ton of style.

Howell: Every unexpected event in life presents Howell with an opportunity for philosophical contem-plation and humoristic endeavour.

Hubert: As a consequence of a very conservative upbringing he has solid and commendable values that stretch toward intolerance. He cleans out his ears, daily.

Huck: In one of those rare events that even the greatest minds that delve into the complicated mathematics of quantum mechanics are at a loss to define or understand, Huck radiates positive ions. So, take a big breath, stand forth, and just walk into him.

Hudson: Hudson is handsome (kind of) and funny (sort of), but he is a brooding egomaniac who eventually gives everyone the shits. What is it with these American names?

Huey: A bumbling good guy who never rushes any-thing.

Hugh: The Hoarder. Whether he's an opal prospector in Coober Pedy, a sculptor of marble or a painter of oil on canvas, Hugh is some kind of artist and he hasn't showered or shaved in years. (Unless he's the Hugh that works on the floor of the stock market, in which case I wouldn't bother with him.)

♂ MALE

Hugo: King Hugo (the full moon) comes out to play for a couple of nights every month and it's him that casts the spell that makes everyone go crazy – and he brings with him one of the great senses of humour. It's his job, after all, and not just anyone can pull it off.

Hunter: Delusional.

Huon: Educated and relaxed, Huon takes his time and rarely gets flustered.

Hurricane: The name of Ryan's cock.

Hutchy: The Great Egyptian Sphinx. No one knows what he's thinking although it's probably pretty good because Hutchy is nothing if not cunning.

Iain: See Ian, although the weird 'i' in the middle of his name provides him with more ego.

Ian: The sound of a teaspoon being dropped onto a tiled floor. The ungainly twang is noisy without being painful and more often than not it leaves a mess, but did you ever stop and study the shape of the pattern of the mess? Check it out next time. You might be surprised to discover the artist that lies within.

Igor: Igor is more light-hearted than you think but do yourself a favour and don't even *pretend* that you want to fight him. It's a Croatian thing...

Ilias: Ilias is a medical name for a medical man in that he computes information very quickly and, by and large, very well.

Indi: Hyperactive.

Innis: Stoic.

Irfan: Irfan excels at finding simple solutions to seem-ingly complex problems.

Isaac: You'll often find his picture in the social pages where he is generally surrounded by beautiful women who seem to be having the time of their lives.

Israel: Quietly spoken and hopeful, Israel is only dangerous when he's riled (or cornered).

Itchy: The highly intelligent and fast-moving gymnast. Perpetually ready for just about everything.

Ivan: Ivan believes that everything in the world exists inside well-defined black and white squares.

Ivo: No, Ivo isn't evil, he's just a man trying to look and act like a man in a world where men are being urged to behave very correctly.

Izzy: As a funny, smart and charismatic bastard, Izzy is irrepressible.

Jack: As one of life's great experiences, Jack is the name given to the phenomenon of a parcel arriving unexpectedly in the mail from a good friend. Outstanding.

Jackie: Funny guy. Loud mouth. Loves the spotlight.

Jackson: Surprisingly bland.

Jacob: The Baptist minister that hails from Vancouver, Canada. Yes, Canada is Boring's idea of heaven but Jacob is originally from India. He has a teethy white grin and he possesses a generous laugh because he's a generous man. Thankyou Jacob.

♂ MALE

Jacques: A typically loud-mouthed, opinionated and arrogant Frenchman.

Jago: The wonderful International Man of Intrigue and Spiritual Enlightenment. He began life as a baby chimpanzee carved out of ice-cream but then he grew up, and his name and character took off like a hang-glider taking flight from the edge of a windswept cliff. Who knows where he's headed but it will be somewhere ethereal. No question.

Jai: Show-off.

Jaimie: Intense and often perplexing.

Jake: Jake has more pornography in his bedroom than any other male. He was once caught masturbating by his mother who burst into his room to find him standing over an upturned TV with his trousers around his ankles, and with Jake the Snake in his hand. He didn't return to the house for days and, yes, he did eventually move out. He now wears a flannel shirt.

Jamal: Jamal is decent fellow and socially adept. What he is skilled at, however, is grasping an opportunity when it arises and slipping through any gaps.

James: A master of disguise and one of the Enigmas. Fiendishly clever, the only thing he won't do is dig holes, although he does loathe all forms of menial labour. Occasionally very serious, rarely flippant and often the funniest person in a room, he always keeps a little in reserve. This is the James' way.

Jamie: Jamie is a young soul and often highly energetic or controversial. (Note: If he smokes a lot of cigarettes then the windows in his house will shake with the volume of his stereo.)

Jamison: Jamison tends to overdo it.

Jan: (Pron. Yarn) Jan lives a streamlined life and rarely is he overweight. His European heritage assists him to be quite direct and so he accomplishes tasks with relative ease, yet he is a relaxed character who is comfortable in all social situations.

Jared: Jared is basically identical to Jarred except that he's slightly more gullible.

Jarred: Jarred is a polite, normal and content young man with a clean soul and a rural background (unless he gets drunk with a group of his male friends, in which case he's liable to fall into the macho pack-mentality of group idiocy).

Jason: Jason is the only creature in the Kingdom to have two completely distinct subspecies...

Jasonicus _thuggus_: Before he became a son of jail, he was a violent criminal who was sucked down one of life's tougher paths, in lieu of the fact that he carries one of the truly mean and irrational tempers.

Jasonicus _raucous_: A highly intelligent and super playful creature who, seemingly often, seems to have a rather wonderful bias in the direction of the latter....at least as far as anyone can tell by just looking. And what a splendid specimen he is.

Jasper: Born to get around corners easily, Jasper is slippery like an eel in both body and acumen, although he arrives with a splendid sense of decorum. Keep an eye out though because if there's an angle yet to be tested then you just wait, he'll find it.

♂ MALE

Jay: Jay is an unusual bloke with an addictive nature and he's so complex that he's nearly simple. He thinks a lot – perhaps too much – but his interest in the various peoples of the world knows no bounds.

Jayden: Relaxed. Intelligent. Complex. Jayden is a funny guy without being the life of the gathering and he's quirky without being a bore. Yep, Jayden does quite nicely most of the time.

JD: (Said with a deep, slow voice)..... "My name's JD... and I like my women... dim and pretty."

Jean: True, it is impossible to take a man too seriously when his name is Jean, and so he had nowhere to go other than down the path of either the nonchalant comic legend, or the unforgiving captain of industry who is famous for getting pissed and wanting to brawl.

Jed: Jed has a resting pulse of 11, he is able to carry a grown cow under each arm and he has a laugh with nearly everybody. Jed, how are you boy?

Jeff: Often covered in concrete dust.

Jensen: The army Corporal who aspires to be a General. On the surface he is a tremendous leader of men but, sadly, he lacks common sense and this makes him incredibly dangerous in a situation where he's in charge of men with guns.

Jeremy: Jeremy is intelligent and ostensibly gentle, but if he's highly ambitious then he can be a slippery customer to deal with. He'd make an excellent head steward for an airline.

Jerome: Rarely visibly excited, Jerome speaks fluent French, Arabic and English and he used to work for the military.

Jerry: The name of a cardboard box that used to hold bananas. He's sort of useful, kind of flexible and semi-interesting if you need to move anywhere but if he sits in the corner for too long you'll forget that he exists at all.

Jess: A baby-faced teenager no matter how old he is, who has a surprising amount of initiative.

Jesse: Jesse rhymes with Mud Brick.

Jester: An unmitigated fuckwit.

Jesus: People stop and take a second when they hear his name, and Jesus is mild mannered as a result – possibly even timid.

Jez: He's no Rhodes Scholar but he's 100% true blue.

Jim: Option A : Brainwashed by society to the conformities of what constitutes a strong male in a rural environment, Jim, while a pleasant and generous individual, is incapable of dealing with highly complex issues. He is a simple fellow at his core, so maybe he's lucky that he lives a simple life.

Option B : Good bloke.

Jimbo: Jimbo is a sensational, goofy and loving man, who would be able to accomplish so much more in life if not for the fact that he has a sheep brain in his cranium, and not a human one.

Jimma: The intellectual and/or physical juggernaut that, like many-a-James, keeps a fair bit in reserve while quietly biding his time.

♂ MALE

Jimmy: Like any decent crap that you're dying to have, Jimmy is bare-boned, rude, proud, occasionally very funny and, generally, wonderful to experience. (Just be careful of the cleanup.)

Jisou: Jisou is an under-the-radar operator. He has the dedication and passion to enable him to stare at a screen/sculpture/mould/garden/duco for hours or days until he is sure he's got it just right.

JJ: Known and loved by hundreds, JJ is exceptionally bright and enthusiastic. One of his few failings is that he is incapable of saying the word 'no'. Whenever he goes out at night, he wears bright silver pants that could have been worn by any famous motorcycle stunt rider. Women adore him until he falls foul of them, at which point they learn to treat him like a lovable little brother. Hate never gets a look-in.

Joakim: Active and tidy, Joakim is an energetic individual whose appreciation of people and place provides a refreshing point of view.

Jock: He might be Scottish and he might not, but Jock is very intelligent, surprisingly sensitive and extremely funny. So long as he doesn't live near any kind of outback mining community, then Jock is a wonderful bloke.

Jocko: Had he decided to become a comedian or actor, he'd be famous by now.

Joe: Joe moves, thinks and speaks slowly, unless he has an Asian heritage, in which case he does exactly the opposite.

Joel: Joel has one of the lowest IQ's in the entire Kingdom.

Joey: In what is considered a miracle of human physiology, while his body kept ageing, his brain and intellect ceased developing at the age of 17. To this day no one is sure if this is a curse or a blessing...

John: John is the name of that huge boulder sitting out there on its own, near the edge of town. He's been there so long that we hardly even notice him any more – he's just part of the furniture. There's a section on the other side of him that hardly ever sees the sun, which may have occasional ramifications, although nothing's perfect anyway, but there he sits. He'll be there long after all these humans are dust and one day he will become dust himself.

Johnno: Mr. Good Natured.

Johnny: When he was young, Johnny went so hard that he nearly went crazy but he finished all of that a long time ago and he has mellowed dramatically. Nowadays, he teaches yoga and he is in touch with the universe.

Jonah: The name topples over itself at the finish like a huge ocean wave crashing over a reef after a journey of a thousand miles and, therefore, there is a sense of tragic beauty about him.

Jonathon: If he isn't either slightly ridiculous or an eccentric tosser, then Jonathon is in the Top 20 most boring people on Earth.

Jordan: Too cool for school. (Again, what is it with these American names?)

Joseph: A serious character who is there when you need him. He frowns more than he smiles but it's probably all a front. He's a good person and far brighter than you'd imagine.

♂ MALE

Josh: Unexpectedly hilarious, secretly competitive and always understated, Josh moves quite slowly – he can't help it – but never without purpose.

Joshua: The sensitive arts student who has many more female friends than male. He desperately wants to win the Archibald Prize.

Juan: Soft-natured like a placid pony.

Jude: Jude is a mellow and sufficiently suave individual but he wouldn't be seen dead drinking at the pub that his identical sister works at, which is a pity. Having said that, if he did, and he got into a fight, she'd be able to defend him better than he would.

Juice: A sinewy little fucker who gets pissed and takes his pants off.

Jules: Friendly. Confident. Playful. Relaxed. Blah blah blah... but he's weird when he's pissed because he can't handle his alcohol.

Julian: Julian plays an instrument and he's okay without setting the world on fire. What he is skilled at, however, is placating angry people and thinking with a political mind.

Jumbuck: The alcoholic stoner who is as irrepressible as he is funny. (And, yes, he's a shearer.)

Justin: 'Justin' is what happens to a bowl of cereal if you leave it to take an extended phone call. Soggy, dull and aesthetically horrific, afterwards, to finish the meal is tantamount to culinary suicide.

Kai: Not dissimilar in nature to Rick, Kai has a ton of energy and a mind that won't easily switch off. He quite literally hasn't got time for enemies as he's continually wondering how he can get to that great spot, just over the horizon...

Kal: An American-Canadian who was born as Karl. He was never that intricate a personality, anyway, but as soon as he rode his first horse it was obvious that the name Carl (or Karl) couldn't be said smoothly while sitting in the saddle at a gentle canter. And that was that; Kal became Kal and to this day he's a good and gentle person. Most animal lovers are.

Kamali: The classy, educated and well-dressed feral.

Kamran: Honourable. He'll blow the whistle if he has to and he'll wear the consequences, because he knows that someone has to.

Kane: The term given to the facial expression of a man who has just been kicked in the nuts.

Kapani: Like the man himself, his name is calm and energetic with a perfect composition. And that's Kapani's secret – it's all about balance.

Karl: See Carl, although this one is generally far more anal and manipulative.

Kayden: A capable lad who generally doesn't wait for life to come to him. Like Jim, however, complex issues may occasionally prove to be extremely problematic.

♂ MALE

KC: ...if only K.C was able to write a story of his life and his pleasures. He has enjoyed the wild and wicked delights of the orient and beyond, his closest friend is one of the unsung iconic figures on the Australian mainland and everyday he wakes up, looks about, and roars with the notion that his master may very well make him famous, today. K.C is the name of Kevin's Cock and I will tell you, ladies and gentlemen, gentlemen especially, that K.C wants to be your friend.

Keenan: Is he a keen man? Probably. He's also ostensibly conservative and pragmatic.

Keith: Keith has a younger brother called Graeme, a cousin called Bill, his Dad is Les and his mother is Violet. His sister is Sheila, his wife is June and he has two children, Brian and Margaret, both of whom have had kids of their own. Keith absolutely adores his grandchildren.

Kelly: Kelly is a quick-witted old bastard who has a fantastically massive gut that he acquired via years of heavy drinking. It'll probably kill him in the end and that's okay by him – he'll tell you that something has to.

Kelvin: Kelvin wears a mullet hairdo, a huge moustache and at a large and hairy 52 years of age believes he's a sex God. And perhaps he is...

Ken: Ken rhymes with Brick.

Kent: As a distant relative of Evan, Kent can keep you awake for hours. Kent....Kent.....Kent, drips the leaking tap. If you don't get up and do something about it you'll get no sleep at all.

Kenneth: Kenneth is the name of the face that every man pulls when he shaves the most difficult part of skin on his face – often it's that bit just underneath the nostrils – and the more ridiculous the Kenneth, the easier it is to get to. There's a trade off in all that we do, after all.

Kenny: Kenny is more lively than his older cousin (Ken) but... what does he do with his time? He always seems to be cruising around but, does he have a job? Where does he go on the weekend? Has he got a girlfriend? Does he have any responsibilities, at all??....Anyone?

Keppler: Despite a flailing mass of arms, legs and elbows, Keppler is an honest performer who does a good job.

Kerry: Far more capable than his female namesake, Kerry is self assured, energetic and well suited to positions of power and influence, although he never sees it like that – he's just having a good time and not wasting any while he's at it.

Kev: The Natural. He can cope with the seventy eight staff that work for him like he can cope with going to bed when he's knackered, no worries.

Kevin: An enthusiastic dunce and the name of any tourist who pulls his shorts up around his armpits and tucks his socks into his sandals.

Kieran: Kieran is a genial fellow who moves easily through the world and without much fanfare, and he possesses an unusual amount of pluck because he understands the benefits of dedicated application. He might even be pretty good with a guitar.

♂ MALE

Khell-ore: (Pron. Shar-loo-vaar) You can't say his name without a mouthful of marbles but he is a relaxed and friendly customer, as are most expat Norwegians. And the complexity of his name in this Australian land gives him great scope to become something out of the ordinary.

Kim: Deceptively lively. Kim doesn't often show his emotions and he scowls a lot of the time in an attempt to convince the world that he is, in fact, a man and he's a staunch realist as a result.

Kimbo: The cat in a human body. Know them and you'll know Kimbo.
(Note: He's the sort of fellow that buys $20,000 worth of shares in a few companies listed on the stock exchange, and then promptly forgets what price he bought them at.)

Kingsley: Kinglsey rides a gallant steed on his expansive estate, thinking that the American military satellites are watching his every move. Good luck Kingsley.

Kirby: Kirby is as useful, artistic and inspiring as a single cucumber sitting on a clean white plate. He is therefore quite unique.

Klaw: Klaw continually itches for a good time.

Konrad: A brand of make-up bag.

Korin: One of the Gifted Ones. True artistry, in any way, shape or form drips from his fingertips.

Kovak: Hungarian. Shy, wild and wise, Kovak is an incredible guitarist. When he plays, it sings of love and therefore forgiveness.

Kung Fu: Asian kid.

Kurt: The Leopard.

Kurty: Sitting at an outdoor table with nothing on but a pair of faded work pants and a smoking fag in his hand, Kurty will only listen to a discussion about what to do if you see a snake within 10 kilometres of the homestead for so long, before he tilts his head back, blows smoke into the air and barks, "Don't be stupid. Just get the fucken shotgun and shoot it."
Discussion over.

Ky: Ky is a young and energetic man at heart who operates inside the bare balls of a situation, which enables him to concentrate on the target. Something like peer group pressure barely registers with him at all.

Kyle: Kyle rhymes with Snide. As a quick aside, 'Kyle' is what you shout after you cut yourself in the kitchen with a serrated knife. Good luck.

Lachlan: Well educated and healthy, Lachlan is a polite man who rarely does wrong by others.

Lachy: Lachy has plenty of friends – both female and male – he never gets morbidly depressed, which means he's a great remedy for those who are, and he does well in any outdoor life where there is plenty of sun-on-skin.

Lance: The Jack Russell that thinks he's a rhinoceros. He expects women to fall at his feet, which they occasionally do, and he has a very mediocre I.Q.

Laird: Hand. On. Cock.

♂ MALE

Lane: Clark Kent minus the superpowers.

Larry: Otherwise known as Languid Larry.

Lau: Picture the God of Neptune in the form of a Solomon Islander chief, enjoying a peaceful snorkel over the front of a pristine coral reef with his two kids following closely behind him. Welcome to Lau.

Laurence: Laurence has spent so much time being proper that those parts of his brain that hunger for thrills and excitement have completely shut down. What is left is a doleful old soul who quietly shuffles around the house in a subconscious quest for the answer to the question of why life seems to be so unfulfilling.

Laurie: That big bloke.

Lawrence: Subtle. Lawrence conducts the London Philharmonic Orchestra and when he's not skiing with the family in Switzerland, he enjoys being whipped by a dominatrix in a Danish dungeon.

Lawrie: If a pack of irrational idiots ever decide to try and beat you up at the pub then Lawrie is a good man to suddenly step from out of the shadows and help out. The idiots, I suspect, would live to greatly regret it.

Lawson: A tall man who stands very straight. He keeps a neat study and gets angry if his highly disciplined children become too rowdy.

Lee: Lee is a straight-up bloke, but he might be a little bit impatient, or something, and there is a 70% chance that he is completely predictable.

Legend: Violent and abrasive.

Leigh: Stubborn.

Len: Len is a chainsaw in need of a decent service. He runs okay and cuts what he needs to cut, but he's beyond the point of being discrete about anything.

Lennon: Watchmaker. Steady hands.

Lenny: Big. Smart. Unpredictable.

Leo: Leo has aspired to be a porn star since he could walk. Indeed, he's so enamoured with his own persona that he sometimes makes pornos on his own.

Leon: One of the great apes. He lives in the jungle, deep in central Africa, he loves bananas and he is completely illiterate.

Leonard: Camilla's betrothed. He's bigger than she is but they smell the same. Ain't love grand?

Leroy: A criminal. He stuffs socks down his jocks to try and make his cock look bigger. He's a funny guy, though, regardless that he spends a lot of time trying to talk to girls from side on.

Les: If ever Les feels tired and lacks the time or desire for a nap, he will stand and face the nearest wall before head-butting a hole in it. That wakes him up, no worries.

Leslie: Leslie is a thoughtful man who, if not well passed middle age, is knee-deep in it. Mild-mannered and inoffensive, he has read more books than exist in a small library and his only real concern is that there aren't many other Leslies left in the wild. If you meet one you should alert the nearest national museum – although there is a slim chance that he may actually work there, already.

♂ MALE

Lester: "....Alright," you smirk. "What's he done this time?"

Lewis: A smart and occasionally intense young man who often seems preoccupied.

Lex: He could be anything on the surface – an ogre or a gentleman – but at his core he is a slippery shit-stirrer who loves a good time.

Lexy: See the female Lexy, although you couldn't really say that the male one is all that beautiful – quite the opposite, actually – and not that he'd give a shit, anyway.

Leyton: Leyton is lucid and contained like an Olympic swimming pool, except that the lanes must be clearly marked, and it would be appreciated if the chemicals in the water react with urine to produce a colour so that the offender can be detected and ejected as quickly as possible.

Liam: Liam is a feisty little bastard that has no compunction in jobbing a man in the face who is twice his size. Sometimes he does it just for the fun of the ensuing brawl. Where's Maryanne when you need her?

Lindsay: Isn't it strange that 'Lindsay' on a woman is quite masculine, yet on a man it's quite feminine? Anyway, the male version hardly ever panics, and this grace under pressure allows him to remain quite methodical amid the turmoil. Such is life, and such is Lindsay.

Linton: A genteel fellow. Quiet of speech, he takes great pleasure in sipping at a nice hot cup of camomile tea.

Lionel: Lionel prefers cold toast in the morning, sherry of an evening, and he takes a long time to do anything. But, seriously, what's the rush?

Lloyd: Lloyd speaks very correctly, collects Jaguar motorcars and wears v-neck jumpers above long sleeve shirts. Unfortunately his permanent ad in the 'Personal' section of the local newspaper seems to go unnoticed, but he hasn't lost faith that a very nice Mrs.Lloyd is out there, somewhere. Good luck, lad.

Loic: His name is actually Gaelic for Louis, and it rumbles passed you like a giant ocean swell as you say it, which makes sense. Loic is the King of the Seas.

Lookaway: Nice guy with a wonky eye.

Lotti: The name of Shirley Temple's favourite little pink dress.

Lou: A middle-aged fellow who loves to dress up in women's clothes more than any other. If he was born in the late 80's he'd now be a transsexual.

Louis: Slick with a line and slick with the hair gel, his life begins and ends with the pursuit of beautiful women.

Lucas: A Lucas is what the dog throws up onto the kitchen floor after it has eaten too many salt n' vinegar chips. Not good.

Lucca: Normally, Lucca is a placid man with charisma and style. If pushed beyond any level of common decency, however, he might snap and become dangerous. He speaks ill of no one unless they're in front of him and deserve it, and he rides a big black motorcycle that, like the man himself, is just as potent as it looks.

Lucky: Supremely Powerful.

Luigi: The motorcycle mechanic who lives in Footscray, in Melbourne.

♂ MALE

Luis: See Louis.

Lukas: His origins are eastern European and he has far more grunt that his Australian male namesake (Lucas). Designed to blend into the background, Lukas gets on with things while at the same time completely ignoring anyone who he considers to be remotely idiotic. (Unless, they happen to be female and beautiful.)

Luke: Luke exists out there somewhere between a fluke and a stroke of genius. He courts disaster with a grin on his face but he can easily fall into a heap if the wind changes direction.

Luther: Far from being as boring as bat shit, Luther plots an intricate course in life and away he goes, out the back door first, usually. Only because he's a stickler for spotlessly clean underwear, and plenty of it. If travelling for more than a few weeks, other than two dozen pairs of jocks, he'll ensure he has three empty plastic bags in which to place soiled linen because under no circumstances would he allow the rest of his luggage to be infected.

Lynden: I wonder if anyone calls him Lyn? Anyway, Lynden is a proper, considerate and well-weighted gentleman.

M: M is a single standing edifice. He's soft in the middle but that matters not. For all intent and purposes, M is a classless leader.

Mac: He was out one night at a club that was full of music, dancing, noise and life, and then he saw Asha on the dance floor. She looked up at the same moment and their eyes met across a crowded room, and it was love at first sight for both of them. What a couple.

Macca: See Noelene, although Macca is far less intelligent.

Mace: His voice is deeper than Bronwyn's although she laughs more. Like Caroline, however, Mace never makes the same mistake twice. And yes, Mace is a man.

Mackie: Mackie the Mackerel Scientist.

Magnus: The name of large, flawless diamond sitting patiently and quietly upon a blue velvet pillow.

Mal: The successful pig farmer.

Malachi: (Pron. Malakai) Ah, if only his name was spelt like that. If Malachi had his shit together then he'd be amazing – perhaps he is not meant to – but like one or two other prodigal sons within the realm, Malachi is wasteful and he lacks foresight.

Malcolm: A chunk of wood about six feet long that's lying on the floor. He's rich in colour, heavy in weight and, how are you Malcolm?

Mango: Friendly guy. Aggressive drunk.

Manuelle: Sketchy.

Marc: The Principal Artist with the Melbourne Ballet Company.

Marco: Marco lost his virginity when he was 8 years old and, having had that much fun as a youngster, he therefore refuses to grow up. Can you blame him? These days he wears tight Speedos and waxes his chest, back, buttocks and testicles.

♂ MALE

Marcus: Marcus is single-minded and cool in a crisis. 'Who is Marcus?' many people ask, and there is a simple answer: Marcus is Marcus.

(In a past life he was a gay New Yorker and his full name was Marcus Maximus.)

Mario: Mario is a hyena that lives a pack existence. Regardless that he might be covered in the blood of a recent kill, he's as funny as hell on a good day and petulant and short tempered on a bad. This is the life, and this is his niche.

Marius: <u>Option A</u>: As a distant relative of the Roman Emperor, Nero, Marius is a predestined leader of men who is skilled at making decisions devoid of emotional involvement. Boring, he may be, but he will tell you that some mild human death and suffering (not to mention plenty of environmental degradation) is a necessary bi-product of any great commercial success.

<u>Option B</u>: Wears hemp clothing. Owns a bead shop.

Mark: Hangs out with Greg.

Marlen: Marlen is an interesting bloke who lives the quiet artists' life. His girlfriends tend to be much younger than him – not to mention physically beautiful – and if he ever gets dumped he knows that all he has to do is relax and get on with life because he always seems to win them back.

Marshall: Organised. Upper-middle class. Thinks he's a bit special.

Martin: A control freak with dark hair. He's not always nice about it but usually he's okay. It's all about money of course and he might question what else really matters.

Marty: The University Prankster who is often short in stature.

MALE ♂

Martyn: The name of the special wheelie chalk machine that is used at Wimbledon to mark the white lines on the centre court.

Marvin: Is it magic or he a magician? No one is certain, but there aren't nearly enough of them.

Masie: Just before he has his photo taken, Masie sucks in a big gulp of air and puffs himself up in the same way a clumsy male pigeon fluffs-up his feathers while in pursuit of another bored female.

Mat: Mat the doormat.

Mataki: A fighter.

Matthew: Matthew is the name of a great mountain ravine up in the Himalayas way above the tree line. Hard to get to, it's an intricately complex place whose difficulty in reaching is matched only be the view that you get once you arrive. Only a select few will ever get to appreciate its beauty but it's an unforgiving environment. If you get injured while you're up there and the weather closes in, then forget it. You're doomed.

Matt: Matt observes the world go by with a natural ease. He is sufficiently outgoing and usually highly intelligent, and he never has too many troubles finding romance, but I'll let you in on a little secret – Matt is so competitive that he borders on being occasionally violent.

Maurice: An Australian aboriginal elder who saw ghosts and laughter everywhere. He's dead now, but as a ghost himself, he still laughs constantly and he still adores beautiful women. Where are you Maur'?

Maurie: Mr. Congeniality.

♂ MALE

Max: This boy is blessed with the letter x in his name that fits in with those around it in an incredibly powerful way. As a result, Max is a wonderfully unusual human being: He is charismatic, sexy and determined, and things just seem to happen when he's around.

Maxfield: A Cavoodle dog (a King Charles Cavalier crossed with a poodle) that is covered in a mop of silky white hair. If he hears a noise outside he'll start barking like crazy before bolting out of the kitchen, whereupon he'll often crash, head first, into the glass sliding doors that he omitted to check were open or not. But the impact never shuts him up for long.

Maxwell: Maxwell has two pieces of toast with vegemite and a big mug of tea every single morning. Loves crosswords.

Maxy: Maxy is thinking all the time, he is discouraged by useless people and dull deeds, and if the world were to be taken out by that giant meteor that Bryce might rattle on about, Maxy wouldn't mind so much, so long as he was standing at the spot where it hit the earth so he could watch.

Mazza: If Mazza were ever to find himself in Hocko's unfortunate position, one fateful night, the only thing he might regret is that he didn't have the peace of mind to think about trying to capture the incident on video.

Melvin: Melvin is a party, and how many names are a party?

Merrick: Merrick rhymes with either Smart Alec or Smart At It. No one is really sure....perhaps it's a bit of both?

Merv: Merv is a good guy who is there when you need him. If Merv goes to the pub for a mates birthday, for example, no matter how many times he himself throws up and no matter how often he gets rejected from entering the disco, afterwards, he'll stick around outside until he knows that the birthday boy has had a good night, and a satisfyingly memorable experience, overall.

Mervin: What is reality? – This is Mervin's personal ethos. Metaphorically or otherwise, Mervin speaks Italian, French, Spanish, German, Swedish and English, he is skilled at metallurgy and wine making and, if attending a large and formal dinner party, he is just as likely to be secretly undoing the $700 bra strap of the Duchess with one hand, while at the same time leading the rest of the table in a resounding rendition from Bizet's Carmen, with the other.

Michael: Catholic school boy. Political advisor/fundraiser. Head engineer. Chief Justice. Airline pilot.....he's in there somewhere.

Michelle: French? Dutch? Maybe. Where ever he is from, Michelle is direct, ambitious and knowledgeable. Is he arrogant? Sometimes. A pain in the arse? Occasionally. Funny? Usually. It depends if he thinks you are a twit or not.

Mick: An Australian icon. He's no rocket scientist – indeed, only physical things that he can touch make sense to him – but his symbol (the fist with the raised thumb) belongs on a flag, somewhere.
(Note: He detests being called Mike.)

Mickey: As an amateur boxer, Mickey has tattoos on his back and shoulders, wears a white singlet, sweats a lot and sports a nose that has been broken at least three times.

♂ MALE

Mike: Mike would make an excellent dentist. He is a calming soul who gets on well with people of all ages, and who understands the consequences of his actions. He feels slightly uncomfortable when people call him Mick.

Mikey: Mikey is usually a big cuddly guy but if he's thin of stature then it's a different story, and he'll be much more suspicious.

Mikle: Mikle is similar to his more affluent cousin (Michael) except that he's never been schooled in any form of theology, his ego isn't anything like the same size and he's probably visited more gentlemens' clubs.

Milan: Milan has a deep voice and he likes to give the impression that he works too hard.

Miles: Nothing like Myles, Miles is an American Tosser.

Millsy: The Gifted Accomplice.

Mirek: The splendid Joker in any deck of cards. His specialty is lewd European trash jokes.

Mitch: Mitch is a gregarious and energetic man. He surfs, he does maths and he has a well- rounded grasp of both the world and his place in it. Like his more unforgiving brother, below, he also knows how to get what he wants although he won't go as far as killing anyone in order to get it.

Mitchell: The Lion Tamer.

Moeseno: The undercover master who is peculiar, honest to the tune of 81% and exact.

Molly: This boy is soft at his core but he is idealistic and reckless on the surface. Gently, gently Molly....

Mop: Mop is a simple fellow but don't be fooled for he is a switched-on operator that has secret plans no one knows about.

Morgan: Morgan carries an attitude that stems from old family money and, fortunately or unfortunately, plenty is expected of him.

Morris: Conservative and stern, Morris has strict moral values. He could probably recite most of the decent psalms from the bible.

Morten: Morten is a calm, quirky and funny individual. As such he is likely to be an investigator of the universe within one of the fields of oceanography, meteorology or nematode worms.

Moses: Moses means well but he's full of himself.

Moscow: There's nothing Russian about him – apart from his love of Vodka – and while he is definitely not normal he looks to get on with life and have as much filthy fun as possible. The last time anyone saw him alive he was being dragged alone into a tent by three gorgeous young nubiles.

Muchy: The wonderful ancient God of mirth, music and profitable betting who can't sit in the same spot for more than about 11 minutes. He's also known as the Host with the Most.

Murray: The Murray is the phenomenon of dropping a bucket that is half filled with mud. After it hits the ground most of it slops straight up and hits you in the face as you stand there. "Oh, Murray!" you cry. He's tolerated in the country, indeed he's very funny, but city folk just don't understand him.

♂ MALE

Muzz: Kinky and thoughtful, Muzz is one of the boys but he's not an idiot, and he's definitely not lacking in available love to give to the world.

Myles: Quietly confident.

Naren: A cross between Norm and Karen, Naren is a contented and humble soul and quite possibly another accomplished artist who is doing his bit.

Nariano: Nariano is one of the few men in the Kingdom who is just about sick and tired of women throwing themselves at him.

Nathan: One of the Achievers. Anal and organized, Nathan's only real problem is that he wears underpants that are too small, which results in lots of frowning when he smiles.

Nathaniel: It probably won't ever happen – I mean, how many people actually get to save the world – but if someone had to, Nathaniel would be a fine contender. Not because he is full of valour and genius for in that regard he's the same as the next person, but because he's a funny, cooky, intelligent melodramatasist whose talents are wasted on the benign.

Ned: Ned slips under the radar as an underrated, genuine and sufficiently hilarious legend.

Negs: The Negs of adulthood is almost identical to the Negs of his childhood. In primary school, for instance, if he and his best mate were being chastised by the female teacher and most of the anger was directed at his mate, Negs would use the opportunity to sneak around behind the head mistress and gently lift up her skirt for a quick peek.

Neil: Neil rhymes with any decent grimace.
(eg: pulling leeches from your skin, ripping the wax from a hirsute part of your body, extracting tropical ticks that have their heads embedded in you and running across 90 degree sand without sandals in order to get to the water.) But, he is a loving man who is true and loyal.

Nelly: A good honest worker who will gladly put himself in harms way in order to save the tribe.

Nelson: A deranged man who yells at non-existent people who are caught up in his paranoid delusions of world catastrophe and bloodshed.

Neo: See Smiddy.

Nev: You'll often find him at the bar of any inland pub on a Friday afternoon drinking with a few of his mates.

Neville: Neville doesn't like what the young folk are doing to the world, and he especially doesn't like their lack of morals and manners. When he visits the dentist to have a tooth removed he refuses to have a local anaesthetic, and there's no way he'd abandon a fruitful fishing trip if he accidentally stuck a hook through his thumb that went all the way through the nail.

Nicholas: A pale-skinned man with the demeanour of a cockroach. People befriend him because they feel bad that he doesn't have any until they realize why he hasn't got any. But, as a gifted shit-stirrer who gets off on testing others, he's highly intelligent and you can't begrudge him that.

Nick: The prodigal son that women are magnetically attracted to. Reckless and irresponsible, he loves outdoor sports and nightclubs, and he understands his place in the world, perfectly. He's never filed a tax return in his life.

♂ MALE

Niels: He might be Austrian, then again his dad might have arrived here on a boat from Denmark, 40 years ago. Where ever his blood originates from, however, Niels is a duty-filled man who devotes himself to any task.

Nigel: It's not Nigel's fault that he has idiotically rude parents, but you can forget the rumours because he is a far nicer and more intelligent person than we were led to believe.

Nikhil: Like a demanding gymnastics coach, Nikhil carries almost unrealistic expectations but you have to give him points for persistence.

Niklas: Greedy.

Nikome: Nikome possesses the resting heart rate of an Olympic distance swimmer and the smile of a contented monk who has been reincarnated so many times that nothing surprises him anymore.

Niz: Serene and truly good (like the fourth of fifth day after earth's alleged creation when there were no animals or humans – just plants) Niz is the quiet calm of the thick rainforest that existed before the maelstrom of animal life and death that came later.

Noah: His name leaves your mouth and swirls around like a puff of disappearing smoke and Noah is therefore hard to get to know, but he is an intense soul who thinks a hell of a lot. (5% of the time he's an artist that lives in St.Kilda, Melbourne, and whose only colour in his wardrobe is black.)

Noel: It happens to men more than women I think, but 'Noel' is the name of the rather tragic splash that occurs whenever a mobile phone is accidentally dropped into the dunny while a person is taking a piss.

Nor: Nor will quite happily walk into a busy pub on his own, enjoy a beer or three, and be completely unfazed whether he ends up speaking to everyone or no one.

Norm: Norm rarely showers, which is a pity because he lives in the heat of Northern Australia, and he only moves quickly when he needs to grab another beer although he'll do anything for anybody, if asked. (He'd never tell you, openly, but he craves the company.)

Norman: Richard's offsider and a fellow knight, who is blessed with no common sense whatsoever. The last time he rode into battle he accidentally stabbed his own horse with his sword as they were crossing a stream. The poor horse died and Norman, the irreverent twit, damn-near drowned in the process.

Nugget: Nugget is the working-mans' ideal of a funny little bastard and if he isn't very short, he's a certainty to have a bright red afro.

Nuts: It's not possible to be called Nuts and not be a humorous individual but the ego, which in this case runs far deeper than the larrikin at the surface, will always get things done in the end.

Oden: The name of a Viking ship sailing the frigid waters of the North Sea. Well made, Oden deals with adversity very well. Indeed, he loves it.

Ohad: Peaceful on the outside. Domineering in the bedroom.

Olar: Rarely loud and 'in your face', Olar measures his words that are well-intended and wise. He's a funny guy, and in past life he was a Great Fish Sage that lived in the Mekong River, in Vietnam.

Old Mate: Cray fisherman. F.N.Q.

♂ MALE

Oleh: Serious when it comes to the family name and moneys owed, Oleh is continually trying to find a way forward.

Oliver: Oliver is serious and sensitive but is it a front? Melodramatic when it comes to matters of love, Oliver in his element when it rains for days on end because it means he doesn't have to leave the house. (He hates direct sunlight.)

Ollie: Ollie is about 40cm tall, covered in brown fur and has little buttons for eyes. Boys and girls talk to him after they go to bed.

Orlando: Pavlova.

Oscar: Option A: An outstanding personality from any angle. He has a thousand jokes and weird anecdotes up his sleeve and the numbers of many more mysterious women in his little black book. He hardly ever works and he gets invited to lots of parties.

Option B: See Radar.

Otto: Peaceful. Humorous. Wise. Affectionate.

Ou: (Pron. Oo-uh) Traditional and Turkish, Ou dances like an alien creature that has just discovered recreational drugs.

Owen: Owen is a round sound for a round fellow, and for a well-rounded individual. He grows organic vegies when he can and a beard sometimes – the former in summer, the latter in winter – and he's married to Betty or Tammy, occasionally Melanie, although that one always ends in tragedy.

Paddo: The Fluid Link Man. Paddo is as knowledgeable and savvy as a sewer rat and he has the weird knack of unconsciously gravitating people towards him.

Paddy: An interesting troublemaker.

Panther: A good-natured idiot.

Parish: The Mysterious Good Guy.
Parish achieves great things but he seems to do it under the cover of perpetual darkness because no one ever actually sees him do anything. How do you do it, Parish?

Pasty: An outboard motor mechanic from Kangaroo Island, South Australia, and pound for pound one of the funniest people on earth. If questioned about his method of feeding his dogs he'll reply with the following statement: "All you do is put out the dog nuts and they'll eat 'em. Eventually they'll keep comin' back. What else can they do?"

Pat: Far more naive than his female counterpart, if Pat isn't a rather innocent kind of fellow then he is thin-skinned. If this is the case then he will try to look relaxed and cool but in actual fact he will complain more than anyone.

Patrick: Never to be trusted, Patrick is a little toy chimpanzee powered by AA batteries who bangs his symbols together for hours, making an irritating, "Patrick, Patrick, Patrick, Patrick," noise, that drives you mental. Later, when he grows up, he becomes a rude doctor with a shocking bedside manner, who gets very angry when the women he fancies don't fancy him back. (Best mates with Martin.)

Paul: Paul is an interesting persona. A polite man whose depths sometimes take years to see, he's intelligent enough, normal enough and he almost never falls ill. To maintain a perfect balance in his life, however, he must perform some semi-evil act every six months. Paul is a deceptively tall name and without some kind of dirty little secret to keep him real, he'd just topple over.

♂MALE

Pauly: Pauly rhymes with Can I Help You? Thus, he's always there, and he'll do anything to help anyone who needs it.

Pedro: Be it in an illicit or legitimate trade in which he's involved, Pedro is prepared to get his hands dirty while at the same time existing in the upper echelons.

Percic: Most men of Adriatic decent are sure of themselves and of their decisions, but cheerful Percic is a little bit different. If questioned about his parentage by somebody in a jovial manner, for example, he won't immediately assume that he needs to kill them.

Percy: Often quite tall, Percy is rarely rattled and his conversations with women are usually risqué.

Peregrine: If he isn't a trifle goofy and light-hearted, then there is an excellent chance he is English, and an arrogant cockhead.

Pero: Pero is a knowledgeable, thinking individual who takes only a moment to size up most situations – lethal or otherwise – and he's always ready to act, holding only as much fear in his heart as he needs to keep him thinking efficiently.

Perry: The bottom button on a shirt as worn by Alastair. He is secretly devastated when he gets tucked-in because he can't see anything and this happens all the time.

Pete: See Peter.

Peter: His name is older than the rocks but he always has plenty of energy, which might explain why he's the butt of many jokes and the cornerstone of many buildings. How did you pull that off Pete? I'm still trying to figure it out.

Peters: As a result of constantly explaining his name properly he has learned to turn everything into a joke, which is handy given his quite ambitious nature.

Petero: Bull at a gate.

Pez: As a bouncer with a degree in Greek philosophy, Pez is a big guy whose dangerous eyes shield a soft heart.

Phil: The Streaker.

Philip: The pompous boring poo-poo man.

Phillip: See Philip.

Pi: If he thought it would do you any good, Pi would tell you that genius is the loneliest ticket in the world.

Pidzy: Film maker. Father. Comedian. Remarkable facial hair.

Pig: Self-assured.

Piggy: Piggy is outgoing and a friend to all, but like many of his colleagues he is a fair dinkum nightmare when he's pissed.

Pissup: Pissup is constructed of sturdy moral fibre and he tells a perfectly intricate story – missing no details whatsoever – that always finishes unpredictably.

Pook: Originally from somewhere near South Africa, Pook is centred, calm and forgiving like an oily flat ocean and the universe thus allows him to do anything he wants. Nice work Pook.

Pope: Pope is the kind of bloke who goes to the Melbourne Cup on his own, knowing no one, and by 5pm is $10,000 up, and best mates with the winning jockey.

♂ MALE

Potsy: One dimensional.

Preston: Here is another that believes that the world was made for them, although Preston doesn't understand why walking around with his thumb up his own arse looks weird. It's his God-given right, after all.

Quentin: One might suspect that Quentin is peculiar and potentially highly uncoordinated, but Quentin's defining characteristic is that he is <u>completely unpredictable</u>. (Note: There are rumours going around, however, that his name is responsible for the Q in IQ.)

Quinny: The word can't be said without smiling and Quinny, therefore, takes very little seriously. Kids light up when they see him, for instance, because, like dogs, cats, crows and most horses, they are the only ones that can see what's really going on - ie. he unconsciously generates an energy field that instantly makes those in his midst feel completely happy.
Weird but true.

Quinn: The Island.

Radar: The name of a pet.

Raechacha: The name of a South Pacific Island dance. You can only do it properly if you are smiling ridiculously, fitter than a Malley Bull, dressed in a islander grass skirt and wielding a spear with the full intention of slaying any bastard who has anything bad to say about you, which obviously never happens.

Ragan: This boy makes clinical decisions, which partially explains why he is so successful.

Rakhal: His name catches everyone completely off guard and they have no choice but to stand up straight and listen to him, out of surprise as much as anything. The wash-up is that Rakhal is a sufficiently unconventional and honourable man.

Ralph: Ralph is an affable fellow who remembers most jokes, and this says everything about his intellect that is huge. If he had an edge to him he could do anything and exalt in the greatness of his achievements, but then he wouldn't be Ralph.

Randal: Randal is a brand new chemistry textbook that ends up spending years in libraries all over the world, and where he gathers dust and meditates.

Randy: He's a unit, alright. Randy is an outgoing bloke who drives a Japanese sports car that has purple neon lights attached to the bottom of it and a souped-up muffler attached at the rear. The muffler is big and silver and, secretly, Randy wants a cock that looks and sounds the same.

Ravi: The Magician. He has beautiful white teeth, he smiles 95% of the time and he constantly thrills thousands of people with the dance parties that he puts on.

Ray: Ray was released from prison about a year ago after doing something silly when he was much younger and far stupider. He came to regret that but, nowadays, having won back the love of his kids, he wouldn't trade any of his history for anything.

Red: Jackaroo.

Reece: Reece is many things - he is a small splinter beneath a finger nail, he is cocky and ever-so-slightly sleazy, he is a good assassin.

♂MALE

Reg: Reg is as deaf as a decent sized post. He says, "What?" so often and so loudly at the nursing home that people have stopped talking to him, outright. As a young bloke, however, he sold combine harvesters and raised a nice family.

Regan: A name for the silver screen. Regan is a sufficiently thoughtful and dedicated man but if you ever implied that his name had a feminine aspect to it, he would probably pick you up by the throat with one hand and gently tear your head from your shoulders, with the other.

Reginald: A pompous English explorer who never knew his east from south. He was only able to do the travelling he did, anyway, because his father had some pull with the government but all was for nought, however, because in 1910, while on an expedition into the mountains of New Guinea, he was eaten by a tribe of cannibals. Apparently his meat was crap.

Reinhard: The Gallant Saviour.

Reini: A semi-successful mover and shaker who knows all the bouncers at all the clubs. And they love him.

Reuben: The name of a mountain stream that is cool, calm and clean.

Rex: Maggie's father. A wonderful old bloke.

Rhett: His name is unique in the Kingdom in that it's the only one that sounds like a motorbike being revved, such that if you say it loudly at him there's a chance he'll jump, but, overall, Rhett is a cool cat who wears unusual shoes. We all have a niche to fill.

Rhino: Big nose. Smart head.

Ricardo: "Hullooooo," he says with a very heavy accent to a lovely young girl. "I think...tonight......you would be liking to make love with me, no?"

Riccardo: Yep. See Ricardo.

Richard: The knight in shining armour with an ill-fitting helmet that badly impedes his vision 80% of the time. He rides a big white stallion that's not dissimilar to that ridden by Cassandra, although his task of riding anywhere quickly is made far more difficult because the horse continually tries to throw him for its personal amusement.

Richie: Richie always has fags on him and is continually on the lookout for mischief. He's an excellent prankster and an excellent second lieutenant.

Rick: Mr. Restless and Mr. Almost Hyperactive.

Riley: Riley has an ego that wont easily lie down and it's something that he wrestles with constantly. He's good looking, he's intelligent and he's charismatic – he knows all this – but he's a compassionate human being as well with a generous sense of stupid fun. The total story may take years to tell.

Rob: Constant like the sunrise and the sunset, his name is heavy with the burden of reliability and normalness that he would love to shun, and very occasionally does. Basically, Rob is a good guy who will do anything for you.

Robbo: Robbo rhymes with Righto, and to that end he is a free-thinking and unselfconscious legend. He's one of the few people on the planet who can pick up a didge' with little or no musical history and make it sing like it's walking on water.

♂ MALE

Robby: Robby had it all but lacking discipline, he realized too late that pure skill was never going to be enough. He's not always a lost soul, although if he is then all is not lost, either, because he makes up for it by often being the life of a gathering.

Robert: Boorish.

Roberto: How can one letter add so much? Roberto's Italian/Brazilian/Mexican or Spanish ancestry have allowed him a certain freedom in that he exists in a land that is surrounded by music, food, women, wine and friends. (Even though he still might live with his parents.)

Robin: Timidity: 70%.
Altruistic tendencies: 100%.

Rocko: Rocko is sweet and gentle like a playful puppy with sharp teeth, and who is all about having the most fun possible without regard to consequence.

Rod: Rod is intelligent and charismatic, and here for this moment. (He might also be sufficiently opinionated.)

Rodney: Quick and clever. Liked by all. Forever the quiet and consummate actor.

Roger: Closely related to Leon, Roger has long arms, is covered in dangly red hair and lives in the island jungles of, what used to be known as, Borneo. He has very expressive lips, he is highly intelligent and as a youngster he's often seen on TV wearing human nappies.

Rohan: Patient and contained, Rohan is the sort of bloke who makes an excellent professional photographer.

Rolan: A Tasmanian caver. He nearly died on a mountain in New Zealand once, but that hasn't stopped him climbing – far from it. And he was the dux of his last year in high school.

Roland: Roland is a graduate of Eton College, in England. He thinks that he is an excellent cricketer and rower, even though has no shoulders, petticoat hands and no hand-eye coordination what so ever.

Rolf: Rolf is a unique and supremely charismatic lover of life. His name sounds like a big dog barking happily at its owner in order to encourage them to toss a tennis ball and, consequently, Rolf has been able to foster his eccentric and artistic ways exactly the way he always wanted....even though that turned out to be a wonderful fluke. Nice work Rolf.

Roly: Roly bustles his portly frame through the door. "Blah blah blah....you wouldn't believe what just happened to me........hey, did you hear about the priest and the donkey?.....Anyone seen my fuck'n lighter?.....What are you pricks up to, anyway?..."
Even watching him is enough to make you tired.

Ron: "G'day love," he says when he walks through the door, exhausted.
"Hi darl'," he hears from somewhere inside the house.

And the stars above track silently behind a brilliant blue sky.

Ronald: As Irma's catatonic brother, on special occasions we'll see him attached to the front of the promotional Carlton United Breweries wagon. After all, everyone loves a dopy Clydesdale.

♂MALE

Ronny: Ronny chuckles a lot and gets on with things and, 25% of the time, at least, he hides his small-scale crimes quite nicely.

Rosario: Firm but kind, Rosario is the Gentle Patriarch.

Rosco: The goofy firebrand and potent rebel, although you'll only ever see his him in action when he's really fired-up about something, which is never that often.

Ross: Take all precaution. Keep a tranquilliser gun trained on him at all times, even if he appears tame, because he might be faking it. You just never know.

Rove: Fast thinker. He moves from place to place, from person to person and from moment to moment so quickly that he is effectively unembarrassable.

Row: See James, except Row lacks the disguises and he doesn't suffer from occasional mood swings.

Rowen: See Rohan.

Roy: Don't be coy Roy, it's okay to be a boy and you'll be surprised how many of them there are.

Ruben: See Reuben.

Rudy: Rudy has two possible outcomes in life. Either he grows big and dumb, real quick, and dominates the schoolyard as a bully, ending up in a highly evolved life of crime and drugs before dying by the sword (having lived by the sword), or he grows slowly under the weight of huge intellect and eventually spends his days and years in his room trying to hack into mainframe computer systems all over the world. (The latter Rudy spent his previous life as a field mouse, the former as a ship's anchor.)

Rupert: As a child, Rupert spent a lot of time getting into trouble without accidentally killing anyone and in adulthood he has carried-on his merry way. He probably isn't super fit, which won't bother him too much, he makes everyone laugh (basically whenever he wants), he's more intelligent than the next bloke and overall he's tremendous fun.

Russ: His name is heavy and curt like a lead weight plummeting to the bottom of the ocean, and so brief and spectacularly uninformative that there was no way he was ever going to end up like that. In actual fact, Russ secretly searches more intently than most, and definitely more than you might imagine from plainly observing him. His ego doesn't run his life and all of us are better off for it. Thanks Russ.

Russell: Russell, the love Mussel, functions as a fish bone that's caught in your throat. "Russell," you splutter. "Russell, Russell!"
But, fish are healthy for you, right?

Rusty: Camps. Surfs. Fishes. Eats. Thinks. Does.

Ryan: The affable tradie' that parties so hard on the weekend he sometimes does himself damage.

Ryder: Good guy. His ego might drive his existence but he is sufficiently cluey and compassionate, and his only really negative attribute is that he is occasionally extremely lazy.

Ryle: Ryle is placid like an old eagle that can't be bothered chasing after the females any more. He's just content to sit on his perch, take in the view, admire the surrounds and generally go about his business of being sufficiently noble.

Salim: The gentle sailor.

♂ **MALE**

Sammy: Sammy is a textbook knockabout lad who cruises along, quite nicely. People are always happy to see him, and he's never deliberately hurt anyone who didn't deserve it.

Sam: The name of the human being inside Humphrey B. Bear.

Samuel: Samuel gets called Sam and Sammy by some people, and his friends kill themselves with laughter when he turns red with anger. Welcome to Samuel.

Sander: No, he's probably not originally Australian but how many of us really are? His Northern European eccentricities make him honest in dealings, easy in company and he is skilled at sliding his way out of a maze.

Sandy: As a retired industrialist who used to deal in rivers of gold, Sandy spends every Friday night in an expensive private mens' club sucking on his sherry and his cigars, divvying out insider's-advice to some of the doting young guns who hang on his every word.

Sanjay: Sanjay has all the moves and he knows most of the answers, and if he doesn't know them he'll perform a short skit in order to jolt his memory, or the memory of others. Alternately, he'll perform a skit in order to entertain all of those people aforementioned, just for the hell of it. Has anyone thought of trying to clone him?

Saul: The tiny marsupial mouse who scurries about in the quiet of the night, going about his business quite happily and very efficiently.

Scooner: The perennial piss-taker.

Scott: Sure, he picks his nose in public but Scott is young at heart, enthusiastic in life and more ambitious than most.

Scotty: A physically active individual, people meet Scotty for the first time and feel like they know him, and this empathy gives him a huge scope for success. His great skill, however, is to keep a cool head when others begin to panic and if you were on an Irene-affected flight, you'd want Scotty sitting next to you so you could swap jokes until you bought-it.

Sean: Sean masturbates a tremendous amount, some-times in public, occasionally in car parks.

Sean: No one can tell you about Sean and so you will have to go and find out for yourself. You'll need to walk up into the hills and seek out that old guy with the dogs. He'll give you some bizarre instructions and a special leather pouch that, hopefully, will contain a strange amulet. Aside from some crazy sounding stories, he might even joke about it possibly saving your life if you are ever confronted by a Laargen ghost. Sounds weird, huh? Anyway, many people have vanished trying to find him but what I *can* tell you is that he is good and remarkable man – *if he is a man.*
(Note: There are rumours that he has human bones hanging from his ears and is over 13,000 years old.....)

Seany: See Seany.

Seany: It's a long story.....

Sebastian: We would expect Sebastian to be a deep thinker, and he nearly gets there. What he is, though, is a complicated and good soul.
(Note: If he has blonde hair he is not from Earth.)

♂ MALE

Sergio: Never shy and often the loudest person present, Sergio expects a lot from people and from life, although he never seems that serious when it gets down to the balls of it.

Setanta: Setanta is what Santa Claus turns into after drinking a bottle and a half of Irish Whisky. (It's the only time you'll see him agro or horny.)

Seth: Just as you begin to say his name it suddenly ends in a twisted mess, which is a similar sensation to suddenly finding yourself in a car that's about to crash into a wall at speed, when only a few seconds earlier you could have sworn you were lying on the couch and about to fall asleep. Very disconcerting.

Shabeer: Muslim. Shabeer's method of jumping from a diving board is to bounce twice, leaping straight up into the air, bringing the knees up to the chest which are clutched with both hands, and then entering the water with the cheeks full of air and a very serious expression on the face. If done correctly the result is a tremendous explosion.

Shane: Darren's mate.

Shannon: Shannon wanders around in a daze of having no idea what to do. Unlike his female counterpart, his name trails off into nothing and leaves you kind of scratching your head.

Sharkey: The funny ratbag who, in heaven, would piss himself with laughter if his death was ever recorded in the Darwin Awards.

Shaun: Shaun deals well in those things that he perceives to be the bare essentials, and this is one of his gifts. He listens to his inner-voice which is usually steady and correct and so, depending on how he is living and where he is in the world, if he deems that he needs to smuggle a cup of hash oil back into the country because he can't bring himself to throw it out, he will use his impressive intellect and take the proper measures to ensure that (a) he doesn't get caught and (b) all of his good friends get a chance to enjoy it.

Shauny: The last any one heard of him was two weeks ago when he left the resort he was staying at in Morocco, apparently without telling anyone. No one knows what he did with the hash oil that was given to him.

Shehan: Shehan has a heritage that stems from somewhere near India, possibly Sri Lanka. His name nearly sounds like he's shearin', which makes sense because he's a straight up fellow who is as honest as he is affable.

Shirl: A slightly more polite version of Jimmy.

Shivers: Shivers is more of a beer man, and he tends to keeps most things under wraps.

Shmucka: The actor's actor who performs even when he's asleep. It's a rare gift.

Shoes: Shoes is the sort of man who attends the funeral of a good mate, and listens to the priest as he speaks of his friend's spirit being released to heaven at the same time a white dove is released inside the church, and stands there easily while the bird flies straight onto his shoulder, refusing to fly anywhere else.

♂ MALE

Shorty: Shorty is a funny guy who is smarter than he looks and who doesn't ever quit.

Sid: Never nasty and rarely dull, Sid gets on well with nearly everyone he meets because he gives them the benefit of the doubt.

Sidney: In a habit that he developed in childhood, whenever he's awaiting the arrival of his supper, Sidney grasps his knife and fork in each hand and bangs them repetitively and simultaneously on the table, shouting, "Yum, yum! Hungry! Yum yum! Hungry!"

Siimon: The sort of man that changes his name.

Silvio: Silvio is another grown-up boy whose enthusiasm is occasionally employed to hold up buildings. He has the capacity to be the world's most adoring friend, as well as your most lethal enemy.

Simeon: Simeon niggles and nestles his way into the 'cool' little nooks and crannies of the artistic world.

Simon: Everyone is a scavenger of some sort but this guy is better than most. The Savvy, Sleazy, Sensible, Sensitive, Selfish and Strong ratios are what is important here, so who can say? Are you Superstitious?

Sisco: Sisco rhymes with "Fuck, yeah!"

Skinny: Like Stretch after him, his physique is assumed except that he is oh-so sensitive. Skinny is on life number 2 and he knows it but, like Rhonda way before him, he's searching desperately for the answers (which probably means that he's actually on life number 5).

Slimey: True to the cause.

Smiddy: If Smiddy is a room full of people then there is only one of them on Earth. I have no idea what would happen to the universe if ever there were two. It might just implode for something funny and cool to do. Who knows....

Smiley: Whether he's about to speak with the Prime Minister or he's in the middle of getting 4 crazy kids off to school, it's difficult for Smiley to get loaded up with the stresses of responsibility. His name catches the world off-guard, which keeps him light on his feet, partially because he is continually on the look-out for anything new; be it weird coincidences, new toys, unusual recipes or undiscovered coral species. (Closet sexual deviant.)

Snap: Pass.

Solomon: The card shark. He speaks in low tones in lieu of all those O's, which rumble in the back of your throat like the ominous rumblings of an over-regulating government. He understands the tax system backwards.

Sonny: The Walking Ego.

Soz: The remarkable cat with nine lives. (Note: He's got about 2 left.)

Spearo: Smooth in water. Ungainly on land.

Spencer: Spencer loves golf clothes despite his inability to play the game. (He has a fetish for fishnet stockings and he secretly wears them under his trousers during competition.)

Spider: Gangly and potentially creepy.

MALE

Spike: Like his namesake on a mathematical graph, Spike is capable of either the best or the worst, and there isn't too much middle ground.

Splinter: Splinter is awkward, hardworking and brave.

Spock: Like his namesake from the Starship Enterprise, he was born with gifts that are often misunderstood by those in the human world. The question is, how will he discover them, and what will he do once he does?

Stamps: The tall, gentle and unflustered man (on the surface, at least). He'd make an excellent fireman.

Stan: Basic. Often miserable.

Stefan: Stefan rhymes with, "Spitting an olive pip out of your mouth that's just cut your cheek and nearly cracked a tooth as you bit into it by mistake."
(Note: Remembering, of course, that olives are tasty and nutritious, and that Stefan's substantial physical and/or intellectual capabilities may one day save your life.)

Stephen: Neat, fussy and often lean or small in stature, Stephen won't wear underpants unless they are properly ironed. By preparing well at every level of his waking life he enables his financial services business to thrive like few others, and he is now quite wealthy as a result.
(Note: Stephen is completely unrelated to Steve, and he feels very uncomfortable whenever anyone refers to him by that name.)

Steven: Steven thinks that only immoral women give head.

Steve: Steve walks a fine line. V is a powerful letter that can provide immediate greatness, depending on where it is, but if too much time is spent on the 'ee' before you get to the V, Steve may well turn out to be a truly sly prick. If it is kept short, however, he can be one of the great individuals. Funny as well. See how you go....

Stevie: Stevie is greasy, slimy and sleazy like a low-grade hustler in Mexico City.

Stewart: An English-styled buffoon who is very polite on the surface.

Stian: The hyper-intelligent loner.

Stinky: Juvenile.

Stirling: A private school ponce who is the first to volunteer to go into battle for King and country, primarily so he can bed the women who are attracted to his uniform that sports lots of little gold tassels and shiny metal bits from when he once blew up a tribe of African natives using cannons. (He avoids walking near primary schools because all the children point at him and yell, "G'day Mr. Peacock!")

Stoner: Stoner is upbeat, energetic and adventurous.

Stretch: Stretch is a good, humorous and reliable individual who kind of lopes along the street in the same way that he lopes along through life. Like his female namesake, Stretch is invariably tall.

Stuart: An upstanding member of society who helps out in community projects, such as Meals On Wheels. His mother insists that he eat Sunday lunch at her house every weekend, much to his initial chagrin, although when the apple pie comes out he wouldn't be anywhere else. And he loves his mum.

♂MALE

Stu: Soft like a sponge, Stu can deal with any situation.
                  He's probably the most adaptable and malleable of
                  all the male species and a better absorber of shock or
                  strangeness does not exist. One day he'll be canonised
                  and we will then know him as St. Stu. And rightly so.

Stuey: Stuey is a lovely bloke who will do anything for anyone,
                  if need be, (which is a product of the softness of his
                  name) and as a trade-off he often lacks a potent killer-
                  instinct.

Sunny: Forget corporate achievement or material gain,
                  for Sunny is powered by a different kind of sun – a
                  connected, hilarious and spiritual one.

Sven: Like a short lick of a potent and over-ripe cheese,
                  Sven has a unique and complex flavour. He's a highly
                  intelligent and optimistic fellow and if you're chasing
                  an intense journey in the name of love or friendship,
                  he could be your man.

Swampy: As an outgoing and loudish-mouthed egotist, Swampy
                  is ideal to have around when a group conversation
                  has become uncomfortably stilted. In this setting his
                  presence will be secretly adored by all those present.

Sydney: Virtuous.

Taj: Silky smooth, laid-back and determined, Taj is nowhere
                  near as soft as he sounds. Indeed, he is an incredibly
                  friendly and intuitive soul who has the world at his
                  feet.

Taki: Shifty.

Tangi: Tangi from the Cook Islands. You want, he get.

Tangles: His reflexes move like a train that has sat on the same piece of line for 30 years and is therefore rusted into place, but he's an optimistic, funny bloke who can lift a shitload of weight, which has to come in handy sometimes, right?

Tay: As a ghost that lacks an actual physical body, per se, he gets extremely frustrated, not to mention very thirsty, whenever he attempts to pick up a glass of water because he can't actually grab the thing.

Taye: See Tay.

Taylor: He recovered quickly after his sex change operation and now headlines at one of Sydney's most popular cabaret clubs; big smile, great legs.

Taz: The reliable and good-natured show pony.

Teale: He's not a duck! He's a snake – a great big lazy rainforest python. He drapes himself over limbs all day and likes to chill-out in the shade. He's a cool customer by default and he rarely looks flustered.

Ted: Ted was a Spitfire pilot in World War 2 and as a very old man with a glint in his eye, he now runs the newsagent on the corner. He's a lovely old man but he was a tyke in his younger day.

Teddy: An older guy who is all fun-and-games until the shit hits the fan.

Tenpa: His middle Asian origins are 1000's of years old, and it helps him to spread the word of peace. (An aggressive temper is something he never has.)

♂ MALE

Teo: A light weight American name, and the title of any individual who gets frightened when someone leaves a door open at the other end of the house, thus allowing a chilly breeze to infiltrate the building.

Terrence: Terrence secretly detests being called Terry, which some people do just to get a rise out of him. He likes fine wine and expensive restaurants, and he went grey very prematurely.

Terry: Terry rhymes with Occasionally Unreliable and, sometimes, Downright Wrong. (His name is short and light like a piece of driftwood.)

Tex: Tex enjoys himself to the point of over-indulgence.

Thomas: Earnest and organised, Thomas has a personality similar to that of a set of architect's drawings for any modern office block.

Thommo: Thommo is tall, friendly and industrious.

Tiger: A Tasmanian Devil.

Tie: Ironically, Tie is the last person to be tied down to a job, a woman or any kind of long-term obligation. Indeed, he is one free man.

Tim: Tim can be a sneaky little bastard or a genuine legend and, irrespective of which, he is highly intelligent and slides around all decisions quickly. By and large he has very good hand-eye coordination and you can be rest assured that once in his life, and only once, will he say to a fool who is pestering him, "You're a mere apparition of humanity."

Timothy: Timothy is an interesting chap. He's quick and he's clean, and he often stands in front of the mirror of a morning, pulls up his Y-front underpants very high around his waist and says, "Morning Timothy!"

Tobin: Kiwi's aren't normal and it's for this reason that Australians barely tolerate them but Tobin is different. Is he the most 'normal', 'sane' and well-rounded of them all?

Toby: A puny lizard that drops its tail at the first sign of danger, before scurrying back into the undergrowth leaving a trail of blood, fear and goo. (Ironically, perhaps, the only really potent Tobys are completely gay.)

Toci: You'll never see him in an office and you may not see him standing in the one spot for too long, either. Boats, deserts, exotic women....these are the kinds of things that Toci finds fascinating.

Todd: Todd rhymes with Oops. Not in a catastrophic way, mind you, more in the, I-forgot-to-feed-the-cat-but-now-that-I've-remembered-I-will, kind of way.

Tom: While rarely a genius, Tom is a truly good person who is ideal in his role as a big protective brother. (Unless he is unusually small in stature, in which case it's a different story, and one that tells of speed and ambition.)

Tommy: Haunted by the demons of self-doubt, Tommy throws himself into life in an attempt to combat them, head on. Consequently, however, he always dies a tragic death way before he had time to grow old and get wise. Poor Tommy, we then say.

♂ MALE

Tony: It's often difficult to know what's going on behind the eyes. He could be a great bloke who is honest and friendly and thoughtful, then again he might be a tall sleazy strip of pelican shit. The more outgoing Tony is, however, the more he tends towards the latter. See how you go...

Tor: Tor keeps it simple 'cause he can. His name evokes images of Scandinavian fjords, smooth running Harley Davidsons and boyish charms, and this is no mean feat.

Torquil: We understand that he is from Earth but not much more than that. What we do know is that he is hilariously funny, even if he's doing something as banal as boiling himself an egg, although no one is sure where he is going or how he intends to get there. At some point we expect he will cease living, and this will be a sad day...

Trav: The Bulldozer.

Travis: Travis is harmless enough but he's a bit silly.

Trent: Tall, blonde and invariably lean from the early years of hard work or hard playing, Trent lives the good life - copywriter, art critic or charter boat skipper - and these days he's a relaxed character who is enjoying life to the full.

Trevor: Ungainly around women and deceptively serious, in general, Trevor never loses sight of his mantra that a fair reward is gained from a fair effort in all aspects of life that matter; cooking, friendship and construction.

Tristan: At the moment of orgasm he yells out, "OH TRISTAN!!! TRISTAN!! GO, TRISTAN, GO!!"

Troy: Troy breastfed until he was 23 yrs old and this has screwed with his head something chronic.

Twiggy: Twiggy doesn't seem to be that bright and he doesn't seem to have that much common sense but he's a humorous bloke who, once in a while, comes out with these little gems that literally stops everyone in their tracks. It might be an observation or an idea, but they're worth waiting for.

Tyler: Tyler spent two years in a rehab clinic trying to kick a cocaine habit that cost him his family and most of his friends. These days he can be seen begging for money near the entrance to most train stations, but it was never his fault. (*WHAT IS IT WITH THESE AMERICAN NAMES??*)

Tyrone: He may be a steroid-sucking gym-freak, a 150kg melted-cheese legend or the local city council mayor who spends $1500 of taxpayers' money, each week, on ladies' of the night, but whatever he does and whoever he does it with, Tyrone operates out there on the fringes.

Tyson: Tyson is a gem. He is the lad at the playground that will try and swing on a monkey bar that is covered in vegetable oil. He is therefore deceptively thoughtful because the harder he hangs on, the quicker he slips off.

Ushun: Frizzy hair. Outstanding energy. He shadow boxes whenever he's standing in any kind of queue.

Usman: Usman is a tranquil man that deals with pressure very well because he has very clear picture in his head of what he wants and where he is headed.

♂ MALE

Vaughan: Vaughan is six feet tall, wears big black sunglasses, a cheap suit (the trousers of which are four inches too short) and is a surprisingly good used-car salesman. He doesn't like ripping off grannies but he can't help it. They're just too easy.

Vasco: Vasco is a slick and super-smart Real Estate agent on the Gold Coast. He wears a fat gold chain around his right wrist that matches the one around his neck, he drives a Mercedes convertible, and he wouldn't change his lot in life if you paid him, which is something that you wouldn't have to do, anyway.

Vedam: The Song of India.

Vic: The short name hides a complex individual. If Vic is bad he's nasty but if he's good he's great. Whichever one he is, however, he prefers the outdoor life, usually, and he's pretty good with most types of engines, and even though he sports a beer gut.

Victor: Victor is the name of a gold plated calligraphy pen that's worth thousands, and who looks excellent when sticking out the top of a breast pocket. He's used by Clints all over the world in order to sign important Dianes.

Vidhano: The Artistic Director.

Vincent: All Vincents are ultra-sensitive souls who wrestle with their own substantial talents and personalities from the minute they draw first breathe. Often overcome with emotion, it's no wonder Van Gough cut his own ear off and topped himself.

Vinni: The Glib Parasite.

Vrasidas: Vrasidas leads by example.

Wade: Wade was a builder for a long time until he discovered that he a lot more fun by staying at home and seeing how much pain he could inflict upon himself by squashing his own hand in a vice. He baits dogs for a hobby.

Wal: Wal likes his meat and three veg for dinner followed by a bowl of ice-cream. He volunteers for the S.E.S.

Waldemar: Like Merlin the Magician, Waldemar is the textbook eccentric genius.

Wally: As the genial head of the local APEX branch, Wally is filled with the deeds of goodness that are misguided only 10% of the time.

Walshy: Bloody funny. Very clever.

Walter: Abused by his wife, Walter speaks very slowly and after orgasm, which is a rare event in itself, he often can't speak for days.

Warren: As a variety of ferret, Warren is pure white in colour when he is clean but, generally, he's a dull shitty brown, he smells odd and he bites.

Warrick: A muscle bound twit who specializes in verbal diarrhoea and offending women.

Wayne: An ingrown toenail that's red and swollen, painful to look at and even less fun to deal with when kicked.

Wazza: Sweet-natured, reliable and irreverent, Wazza lives for embarking on adventures with his friends.

Webby: Never underestimate Webby. His simplicity is actually cohesion, not confusion.

♂ MALE

Welchy: Welchy gets injured all the time and frowns whenever he's in pain, which is quite a lot, unfortunately, but he is a fun-loving legend who lives his life in his jocks.

Wendell: (Ancestor of Bruce.) Back in the dark ages, in Europe, invading forces would attempt to bust open the gates of a castle with a giant log carried by twenty men or more, who would slam it repeatedly against them. In the absence of any smashing device, however, they'd just grab Wendell, pick him up side-on, and crunch his tremendously large and dense cranium against the gates, instead. It never really bothered Wendell because all he knew of it was a rather loud knocking noise.

Wes: Wes is a big bloke. He knows how to fight a fire, he's familiar with nearly every part of most old utes, he's handy with a welder, he can defend himself, he makes people laugh and at the end of a long day, or even during an annual local festival, he loves a good, cold Australian beer. G'day Wes.

Wesley: The Wesley Treatment is what happens to anything – sandwiches and packs of soft drink cans, for example – when it is wrapped tightly in clear plastic film.

Whacky: (If only he was so lucky.) Whacky is intelligent and methodical.

Will: Will is almost too nice for his own good. He rushes to the aid of all and everyone and he probably should have been an ambulance driver.

William: A sage who has seen and done it all; war, love, family, everything. Now that he's an old man he likes to sit outside in the morning sun, where he reads the paper and quietly reminisces about his wonderful life that is coming to a close.

Willie: A well-intended drip.

Woggy: Woggy = Flash Gordon.

Wolfgang: Petrochemical engineer.

Woody: Woody is rock solid and another comic genius. He loves women and he loves his life.

Woolfy: Woolfy is that cheeky prick who itches for a bit of chaos.

Xavier: A private school boy and all round nice guy. He won't set the world on fire but he won't bore us to death either. Probably.

Yoey: Yoey approaches life like a skimming stone that is 4-bounces into a perfect 9-bounce performance. Question: What's possible? Answer: Everything.

Yong: Yong performs autopsies in the name of forensic science.

Youcef: If you think Youcef is useless you can leave the room for he is a dedicated, animated liver of life whose courage and honour could teach many within the Kingdom a valuable lesson or two. His only real fault, if you can call it that, is that he might occasionally smother people with love.

Zac: Zac is the name of a bright red balloon at a birthday party that was full of air about 7 hrs ago, but now has a few slack wrinkles all over it. A nice guy. A nice balloon. Zac is (and was) a splendid mischief maker and when it counted he was very good.

♂ MALE

Zachary: The poor bastard. His parents gave him that name because they thought it would be a cool thing to do, but they might as well have called him Seventy Cents Worth of Chips, as no one can ever take him seriously.

Zamika: Utterly loveable and completely unconventional, Zamika is always relaxed, and no matter how stressed or panicked those around him appear to be. It's a product of having an unyielding sense of humour, courtesy of a ridiculous mother, combined with an ingrained sense of wrong and right.

Zane: Zane is the name of an expensive pane of glass in a plush modern apartment. He lets in all the winter sun and keeps out the summer heat, and all that, and he does it pretty easily. And he looks good. Yep. That's about it. He looks good.

Ziggy: The Patriotic Hippy.

Zoc: His name sounds like an axe cutting into a heavy log and this isn't far from his measure. The quickness of his title conceals the lengths that he'll go to, to elucidate the truth. And that's why he's here. What a tremendous, searching individual.

Zorba: This man lives a life that is akin to a male detective character in a cartoon book. At one stage he had $80,000 in a shoebox in his bedroom. No one knows how he accrued it – Zorba seems to find himself in these sorts of situations all the time, although he has a lot more stashed in a Swiss bank account – but I suppose it's the natural result of being quite a remarkable personality (not to mention another sexual deviant).

ACKNOWL-EDGEMENTS

I would like to thank the following people for their direct assistance with this compilation.

Mr. Tim Fountain of Hobart, Tasmania, for his Tiger snake-inspired, if not accidental addition for Dante's inferno. Proof, again, that truth is stranger than fiction.

Captain R.B Hortle and his magnificent throng, Dr. L.D Smith, Burkey, Kimbo, Charlotte, Dr. S. Field, Dr. J. Gilmour, Muchy and Zoc. Not forgetting Princess, Ruth, Boss and my good friend, Mr Splash Ontario.

Dr SJ. Pell, how do you do it? Thank you.

And, indirectly, I'd like to thank everyone I have ever met or heard about - dead or alive. Most of you are in here, somewhere.

Lastly, I'd like to thank the staff at VIVID Publishing for their unwavering support, both technical and philosophical.

DISAPPOINTED THAT 'CLINT', THE BOOK, DOESN'T FIT IN YOUR POCKET? FEAR NOT, FOR IT'S NOW A SMART PHONE APPLICATION.

NAME GURU (US $1.99) available now for iphone/ipad, with the Android version coming soon!

FEATURES OF THE APP:

• It lists every name theory that exists in the book (plus a few extras!)

• The shuffle function allows you to select names at random, which is great fun at parties.

• If you're looking for love or just plain curious for the fun of it, the new compatibility function of the app allows you to select any two names from the list and, using a secret system, it will tell you how romantically suited they are for each other!

...And you thought the book was weird??

Printed in Australia
AUOC02n0726101015
270881AU00008B/14/P

9 780980 545937